The Selected Works of Edward Carpenter
First Prism Key Press Edition 2012

Prism Key Press
New York, NY 10001
PrismKeyPress.com

ISBN-13: 978-1468056174

The Selected Works of Edward Carpenter

CONTENTS

England's Ideal

While it seems to be admitted now on all hands that the Social condition of this country is about as bad as it possibly can be, and while many schemes, more or less philanthropic or revolutionary, are proposed for its regeneration, it just occurs to me to bring forward the importance of mere *personal* actions and ideals as in a sense preceding all schemes, and determining whether they are to ripen to any fruitful end or not. For as the nation is composed of individuals, so the forces which move the individual, the motives, the ideals which he has in his mind, are, it seems to me, the main factors in any nation's progress and the things which ultimately decide the direction of its movement.

Not that I wish for a moment to throw cold water on schemes; but that I think we are apt to forget that these are, properly speaking, only the expressions and results of things which lie deeper, and that these deep-seated ideals which lurk more or less hidden in the minds of all of us are in reality tremendous forces, of the very most practical importance, and not mere sentimental matters at all.

To take an instance of what I mean. While we are met on all sides by descriptions of the desperate poverty of huge masses of the people in nearly every civilised (?) country of the world, and are inundated with recipes for their redemption, the simple fact remains and comes out clearer the more one looks into the matter that the cry is in the first place a cry for Justice and personal Honesty, and in the second place only, for Social Re-organisation. At the bottom, and behind all the elaborations of economic science, theories of social progress, the changing forms of production, and class warfare, lies the fact that the old ideals of society have become corrupt, and that this corruption has resulted in dishonesty of life. It is this dishonesty of personal life which is becoming the occasion of a new class war, from whose bloody parturition struggle will arise a new ideal-destined to sway human society for many a thousand years, and to give shape to the forms of its industrial scientific and artistic life?[1]

Say that to-day the gospel of mere personal honesty spread through society, so that it became disgraceful for a man to receive the gift of the labour of others without giving an equivalent amount of his own labour in return; say that only such an obvious and fundamental truth as this were – by some vivid contagion of feeling and influence, such as has marked great historical movements – to spread through all classes; in that instant, need I say it, Society would begin to undergo a magical transformation. Not many more Royal Commissions would be needed, nor bluebooks, nor Mansion House charity funds, nor recipes of benevolent capitalists and philanthropists; somehow the blackened walls of our fever-stricken city dens would crumble and convey themselves away, giving place to homes of cleanly, decent, cheerful life; the haggard sunken-eyed babes that now crawl uncared for into the gutter would be exchanged for laughing ruddy-cheeked children, smiling an unconscious greeting upon the passer-by; and though this one matter might not cure *all* evils, yet I venture to say that if it were attended to this England of ours would, in a few years, be changed almost .past recognition, and from being the sorrowing poverty-stricken country that it is, would claim once more to be called "Merry England" as of old. The new standard, in fact, of personal honesty of life would revolutionise the nation from within, and new forms and a new organisation of society would spring from it as naturally and infallibly as the systematic beauty of a plant springs from the single and undivided seed.

Let us go straight to the point, then. Let us seize at once the inward principles of national life and growth. The question of the condition of our country comes home to each of us ultimately as one from which we cannot escape by the mere elaboration of new laws and new schemes. The new laws and schemes truly must be elaborated, but the personal question must come first.

The feeling seems to be spreading that England stands to-day on the verge of a dangerous precipice. And so I believe she does; at any moment the door may open for her on a crisis more serious than any in her whole history. Rotten to the core, penetrated with falsehood from head to foot, her aristocracy emasculated of all manly life, her capitalist classes wrapped in selfishness, luxury and self-satisfied philanthropy, her Government offices – army, navy and the rest – utterly effete, plethoric, gorged (in snake-like coma) with red tape,[2] her Church sleeping profoundly-snoring aloud, her trading classes steeped in deception and money greed, her labourers stupefied with overwork and beer, her poorest stupefied with despair, there is not a pain which will bear examination, not a wheel in the whole machine which will not give way under pressure. The slightest disturbance now and the wheels will actually cease to go round: the first serious strain – European or Eastern war – and the governing classes of England will probably succumb disgracefully. And then – with an exhausting foreign war upon us, our foreign supplies largely cut off, our own country (which might grow ample food for its present population) systematically laid waste and depopulated by landlords; with hopeless commercial depression, stagnation at trade, poverty, and growing furious anarchy – our position will easier be imagined than described, but perhaps easiest left unimagined.

India – with its "forty millions always on the verge of starvation" – the playground of the sons of English capitalists – must go. Ireland that has nobly struck the note of better things to all Europe, but who in her long and glorious battle for freedom has received no encouragement from the English people, will desert us. We shall call to her for help, but there shall be no answer – but derision. Egypt will curse the nation of Bondholders.

In the face of these considerations let us, as I have said, go straight to the heart of the matter. Let us, let all who care or hold ourselves in any way responsible for the fate of a great nation, redeem our lives, redeem the life of England, from this curse of dishonesty. The difficulty is that to many people – and to whole classes – mere honesty seems such a small matter. If it were only some great Benevolent Institution to recommend! But this is like Naaman's case in the bible: to merely bathe in the Jordan and make yourself clean – is really too undignified!

But the disease from which the nation is suffering is dishonesty; the more you look into it the clearer you will perceive: that this is the source of all England's present weakness corruption and misery; and honesty and honesty alone will save, her, or give her a chance of salvation. Let us confess it. What we have all been trying to do is to live at the expense people's labour, without giving an equivalent of our labour in return. Some succeed, others only try; but it comes to much the same thing.

Let a man pause just for once in this horrid scramble of modern life, and ask himself what he really consumes day by day of other people's labour – what in the way of food, of clothing, of washing, scrubbing, and the attentions of domestics, or even of his own wife and children – what money he spends in drink, dress, books, pictures, at the theatre, in travel. Let him sternly, and as well as he may, reckon up the sum total by which he has thus made himself indebted to his fellows, and then let him consider what he creates for their benefit in return. Let him strike the balance. Is he a benefactor of society? – is it quits between him and his countrymen and women ?-or is he a dependent upon them, a vacuum and a minus quantity? – a beggar, alms-receiver, or thief.

And not only What is he? but What is he trying to be? For on the Ideal hangs the whole question. Here at last we come back to the root of national life. What the ideal cherished by the people at large is, that the nation will soon become. Each individual man is not always *able* to realize the state of life that he has in his mind, but in the nation it is soon realised; and if the current ideal of individuals is to *get* as much and *give* as little as they can, to be debtors of society and alms-receivers of the labour of others, then you have the spectacle of a nation, as England to-day, rushing on to bankruptcy and ruin, saddled with a huge national debt, and -converted into one gigantic Workhouse and idle shareholders' Asylum. (Imagine a lot of people on an Island – all endeavouring to eat other people's dinners, but taking precious care not to provide any of their own – and you, will have a picture of what the "well-to-do" on this island succeed in doing, and a lot of people not well-to-do are trying to arrive at).

For there is no question that this *is* the Ideal of England to-day – to live dependent. on others, consuming much and creating next to nothing[3] – to occupy a spacious house, have servants ministering to you, dividends converging from various parts of the world towards you, workmen handing you the best part of their *labour* as profits, tenants obsequiously bowing as they disgorge their rent, and a good balance at the bank; to be a kind of human sink into which, much flows but out of which nothing ever comes – except an occasional putrid whiff of Charity and Patronage – this, is it not the thing which we have before us? which if we have not been fortunate enough to attain to, we are doing our best to reach.

Sad that the words lady and gentleman – once nought but honourable – should now have become so soiled by all ignoble use. But I fear that nothing can save them. The modern Ideal of Gentility is hopelessly corrupt, and it must be Our avowed object to destroy it.

Of course, among its falsities, the point which I have already alluded to is the most important. It is absolutely useless for the well-to-do of this country to talk of Charity while they are abstracting the vast sums they do from the labouring classes, or to pretend to alleviate by philanthropic nostrums the frightful poverty which they are *creating wholesale by their mode of life*. All the money given by the Church, by charity organisations, by societies, or individuals, or out of the rates, and all the value of the gratuitous work done by country gentlemen, philanthropists and others, is a mere drop: in the ocean compared with the sums which these same people and their relatives abstract from the poor, under the various legal pretences of interest, dividends, rent, profits, and state-payments of many kinds. "They clean the outside of the cup and platter, but within they are full of *extortion* and *excess*."

If for every man who consumes more than he creates there must of necessity be another man who has to consume less than he creates, what must be the state of affairs in that nation where a vast class – and ever vaster becoming – is living in the height of unproductive wastefulness? obviously another vast class – and ever vaster becoming – must be sinking down into the abyss of toil, penury and degradation. Look at Brighton and Scarborough and Hastings and the huge West End of London, and the polite villa residences which like unwholesome toadstools dot and disfigure the whole of this great land. On *what* are these "noble" mansions of organised idleness built except upon the bent back of poverty and lifelong hopeless unremitting toil. Think! you who live m them, *what* your life is, and upon what it is founded.

As far as the palaces of the rich stretch through Mayfair and Belgravia and South Kensington, so far (and farther) must the hovels of the poor inevitably stretch in the opposite direction. There is no escape. It is useless to talk about better housing of these unfortunates unless you strike at the root of their poverty; arid if you want to see the origin and explanation of an East London rookery, you must open the door and walk in upon some fashionable dinner party at the West End; where elegance, wealth, ease, good grammar, politeness, and literary and sentimental conversation only serve to cover up and conceal a heartless mockery – the lie that it is a fine thing to live upon the labour of others. You may abolish the rookery, but if you do not abolish the other thing, the poor will only find some other place to die in; and one room, in a sanitary and respectable neighbourhood will serve a family for that purpose, as well as a whole house in a dirtier locality. If this state of affairs were to go on long (which it won't do) England would be converted, as I have said, into one vast Workhouse and pauper Asylum, in which rows of polite paupers surrounded by luxuries and daintily fed, would be entirely served and supported by another class – of paupers unable to get bread enough to eat!

But the whole Gentility business is corrupt throughout and will not hear looking into for a moment. It is incompatible with Christianity; it gives a constant lie to the doctrine of human brotherhood.

The wretched man who has got into the toils of such a system must surrender that most precious of all things – the human relation to the mass of mankind. He feels a sentimental sympathy certainly for his "poorer brethren;" but he finds that he lives in a house into which it would be simply an insult to ask one of them; he wears clothes – in which it is impossible for him to do any work of ordinary usefulness. If he sees all old woman borne down by her burden in the street he can run to the charity organisation perhaps and get an officer to enquire into her case – but he cannot go straight up to her like a *man,* and take it from her on to his own shoulders; for he is a *gentleman* and might soil his clothes! It is doubtful even whether – clothes or no clothes, old woman or no old woman – he could face the streets where he is known with a bundle on his shoulders; his dress is a barrier to all human relation with simple people, and his words of sympathy with the poor and suffering are wasted on the wide air while the flash of his jewellery is in their eyes.

He finds himself among people whose constipated manners and frozen speech are a continual denial of all natural affection – and a continual warning against offence; where to say 'onesty is passable, but to say 'ouse causes a positive congestion; where human dignity is at such a low ebb that to have an obvious patch upon your trousers would be considered fatal to it; where manners have reached (I think) the very lowest pitch of littleness and *niaiserie*; where human wants and the sacred facts, sexual and other, on which human *life* is founded,

13

are systematically ignored; where to converse with a domestic at the dinner table would be an unpardonable breach of etiquette; where it is assumed as a matter of course that you do nothing for yourself – to lighten the burden which your presence in the world necessarily casts upon others; where to be discovered washing your own linen, or cooking your dinner, or up to the elbows in dough on baking day, or helping to get the coals in, or scrubbing your own floor, or cleaning out your privy, would pass a sentence of lifelong banishment on you; where all dirty work, at least such work as is considered dirty by the "educated" people in a household is thrust upon young and ignorant girls; where children are brought up to feel far more shame at any little breach of social decorum – at an "h" dropped,[4] or a knife used in the wrong place at dinner, or a wrong appellative given to a visitor – than at glaring acts of selfishness and uncharitableness.

In short the unfortunate man finds himself in a net of falsehoods; the whole system of life around him is founded on falsehood. The pure beautiful relation of Humanity, the sacred thing in all this world, is betrayed at every step. Democracy with its magnificent conception of inward and sacramental human equality, can only be cherished by him the hidden interior of his being; they can have no real abiding place in his outward life.

And when he turns to the sources from which his living is gained, he only flounders from the quagmire into the bog. The curse of dishonesty is upon him; he can find no bottom anywhere.

The interest of his money comes to him he knows not whence; it is wrung from the labour of someone – he knows not whom. His capital is in the hands of railway companies and his dividends are gained in due season – but how? He dares not enquire. What have companies, what have directors and secretaries and managers, to do with the question whether *Justice* is done to the workmen, and when did a share-holder

14

ever rise up and contend that dividends ought to be less and wages more? (I met with a case once in a report: but he was hissed down.)

His rents come to him from land and houses. Shall he go round and collect them himself? No, that is impossible. This farmer would show him such a desperate balance sheet, that widow would plead such a piteous tale, this house might be in too disgraceful a state, and entail untold repairs. No, it is impossible. He must employ an agent or steward, and go and live at Paris or Brighton, out of sight and hearing of those whose misfortunes might disturb his peace of mind; – or put his money affairs entirely in the hands of a solicitor. *That* is a good way to stifle conscience.

Money entails duties. How shall we get the money and forget the duties? Voilà the great problem! But we cannot forget the duties. They cark unseen.

He has lent out his money on mortgage. Horrid word that, "mortgage!" – "foreclosure," too! – sounds like clutching somebody by the throat! Best not go and see the party who is mortgaged ;-might be some sad tale come out. Do it through a solicitor, too, and it will be all right.

Thus the unfortunate man of whom I have spoken finds that turn where he may the whole of his life, his external life, rests on falsehood. And I would ask you, reader, especially well-to-do and dividend-drawing reader, *is* this – this picture of the ordinary life of English gentility – your Ideal of life? or is it not? For if it is do not be ashamed of it, but please look it straight in the face and understand *exactly* what it means; but if it is not, then come out of it! It may take you years to *get* out; certainly you will not shake yourself free in a week, or a month, or many months, but still, – Come out!

And surely the whole state of society which is founded on this Ideal, however wholesome or fruitful it may have once been, *has* in these latter days (whether we see it or not) become quite decayed and barren and corrupt. It is no good disguising the fact; surely much better is it that it should be exposed and acknowledged. Of those who are involved in this state of society we need think no evil. They are our brothers and sisters, as well as the rest; and oftentimes, consciously or unconsciously, are suffering, caught in its toils.

Why to-day are there thousands and thousands throughout these classes who are weary, depressed, miserable, who discern no object to live for; who keep wondering whether life is worth living, and writing weary dreary articles in magazines on that subject? Who keep wandering from the smoking room of the club into Piccadilly and the park, and from the park into picture galleries and theatres; who go and "stay" with friends in order to get away from their own surroundings, and seek "change of air," if by any means that may bring with it a change of interest in life? Why, indeed? Except because the human heart (to its eternal glory) *cannot* subsist on lies; because (whether they know it or not) the deepest truest instincts of their nature are belied, falsified at every turn of their actual lives: and therefore they are miserable, therefore they seek something else, they know not clearly what.

If looking on England I have thought that it is time this Thing should come to an end, because of the poverty-stricken despairing multitudes who are yearly sacrificed for the maintenance of it, and (as many a workman has said to me) are put to a *slow death* that it may be kept going, I have at other times thought that even more for the sake of those who ride in the Juggernauth car itself, to terminate the hydra-headed and manifold misery which lurks deep down behind their decorous exteriors and well-appointed surroundings, should it be finally abolished.

Anyhow it *must* go. The hour of its condemnation has struck. And not only the false Thing. I speak to you, working men and women of England, that you should no longer look to the ideal which creates this Thing – that you should no longer

16

look forward to a day when you shall turn your back on your brothers and sisters, and smooth back white and faultless wristbands – living on their labour! but that you should look to the new Ideal, the ideal of social, brotherhood, and of honesty, which as surely as the sun rises in the morning shall shortly rise on our suffering and sorrowing country.

But I think I hear some civilisee say, "Your theories are all very well, and all about honesty and that sort of thing, but it is all quite impracticable. Why, if I were only to consume an equal value to that which I create I should never get on at all. Let alone cigars and horses and the like, but how about my wife and family? I don't see how I could possibly keep up *appearances*, and if I were to let my position go, all my usefulness (details not given!) would go with it. Besides, I really don't see how a man *can* create enough for all his daily wants. Of course, as you say, there, must be thousands and millions who are obliged to do so, and *more* (in order to support us), but how the deuce they live I cannot imagine – and they *must* have to work awfully hard. But I suppose it is their business to support us, and I don't see how civilisation would get on without them, and in return of course we keep them in order you know, and give them *lots* of good advice!"

To all which I reply "Doubtless there is something very appalling in the prospect of actually maintaining oneself – but I sincerely believe that it is possible. Besides would not you yourself think it very interesting just to try – if only to see what you would dispense with if you had to do the labour connected with it – or its equivalent? If you had to cook your own dinner for instance -"

"By Jove! I believe one would do without a lot of sauces, and side dishes!"

"Or if you had to do a week's hard work merely to get a new coat -"

"Of course I should make the old one do – only it would become so beastly unfashionable."

That is about it. There are such a *lot* of things which we could do without – which we really don't want – only, and but ...!

And rather than sacrifice these beloved on lies and buts, rather than snip off a few wants, or cut a sorry figure before friends, we rush on with the great crowd which jams and jostles through the gateway of Greed over the bodies of those who have fallen in the struggle. And we enjoy no rest, and our hours of Idleness when they come are not delightful as they should be. For they are not free and tuneful like the Idleness of a ploughboy or a lark, but they are clouded with the spectral undefined remembrance of those at the price of whose blood they have been bought.

As to the difficulty of maintaining oneself, listen to this, please; and read it slowly: – "For more than five years I maintained myself thus solely by the labour of my hands; and I found that by working about six weeks in a year I could meet all the expenses of living."

Who was it wrote these extraordinary words?

It has for some time been one of the serious problems of Political Economy to know how much labour is really required to furnish a man with ordinary necessaries. The proportion between labour and its reward has been lost sight of amid the complexities of modern life; and we only know for certain that the ordinary wages of manual labour represent very much less than the value actually created.

Fortunately for us, however, about forty years ago a man thoroughly tired of wading through the bogs of modern social life had the pluck to land himself on the dry ground of actual necessity. He squatted on a small piece of land in New England, built himself a little hut, produced the main articles of his own

18

food, hired himself out now and then for a little ready money, and has recorded for us, as above, the results of his experience. Moreover, to leave no doubt as to his meaning, he adds: "The whole of my winters as well as most of my summers I had free and clear for study." (He was an author and naturalist.)

The name of this man was Henry Thoreau. Anyone who obtains his book "Walden"[5], will see for himself the details of the experiment by which he proved that a man can actually maintain himself and have abundant leisure besides! And this, too, even under circumstances of considerable disadvantage; for Thoreau isolated himself to a great extent from the co-operation of his fellows, and had to contend single-handed with Nature in the midst of the woods where his crops were sadly at the mercy of wild creatures. It is true, as I have said, that he had built himself a hut and had 2 or 3 acres of land to start with – but what a margin does his 6 weeks in a year leave for critical subtractions!

If anyone however doubts the truth of the general statement contained in the last paragraph, his doubt must surely be removed by a study of the condition of life in England in the 15th century. At that time, between the fall of the feudal barons and the rise of the capitalists and landlords, there was an interval during which the workers actually got something like their due, and were not robbed to any great extent by the classes above them. A comparison of wages and prices shows that at that time an ordinary labourer would receive the value of from 100 to 150 eggs for an ordinary day's work, and the worth of a good fat sheep for about three day's toil. Now it is not probable that hens are more averse to laying now than they were then, nor is our country at present so overgrazed and cultivated as to increase the difficulty of raising beasts and crops (on the contrary it is half-deserted and *under*-cultivated); it is also certain that the labourer in the 15th century did not receive *more* than what he might be said to have created by his labour; yet the labourer to-day does not get anything like that reward. And the reason is obvious. His labour is as fruitful as ever; but the greater part of its produce – its reward – is taken from him.

As fruitful as ever? – far more fruitful than ever; for we have taken no account of the vast evolutions of machinery. What that reward would be, under our greatly increased powers of production – if it were only righteously distributed – we may leave to be imagined.

As to Thoreau the real truth about him is that he was a thorough economist. He reduced life to its simplest terms, and having, so to speak, labour in his right hand and its reward in his left, he had no difficulty in seeing what was worth labouring for, and what was not, and no hesitation in discarding things that he did not think *worth* the time or trouble of production.

And I believe myself that the reason why he could so easily bring himself to do without these things, and thus became free – "presented with the freedom" of nature and of life – was that he was a thoroughly educated man in the true sense of the word.

It seems to be an accepted idea nowadays that the better educated anyone is the more he must require. "A ploughman can do on so much a year, but an educated man – O quite impossible!"

Allow me to say that I regard this idea as entirely false. First of all, if it *were* true, what a dismal prospect it would open out to us! The more educated we became the more we should require for our support, the worse bondage we should be in to material things. We should have to work continually harder and harder to keep pace with our wants, or else to trench more and more on the labour of others; at each step the more complicated would the problem of existence become.

But it is entirely untrue. Education does not turn a man into a creature of blind wants, a prey to ever-fresh thirsts, and desires – it brings him *into relation with the world around him*. It enables a man to derive pleasure and to draw sustenance from a thousand common things which bring neither joy nor

20

nourishment to his more enclosed and imprisoned brother. The one can beguile an hour anywhere. In the field, in the street, in the workshop he sees a thousand things of interest. The other is bored, he must have a toy – a glass of beer or a box at the opera – but these things cost money.

Besides the educated man, if truly educated, has surely more resources of skilful labour to fall back upon – he need not fear about the future. The other may do well to accumulate a little fund against a rainy day.

It is only to education commonly so-called – the false education – that these libels apply. I admit that to the current education of the well-to-do they do apply, but that is only or mainly a cheap-jack education, an education in glib phrase, grammar, and the art of keeping up appearances – and has little to do with bringing anyone into relation with the real world around him – the real world of Humanity, of honest Daily Life, of the majesty of Nature, and the wonderful questions and answers of the soul which out of these are whispered on everyone who fairly faces them.

Let us then have courage. There is an Ideal before us, an ideal of Honest Life – which is attainable, not very difficult of attainment, and which true Education will help us to attain to, not lead us astray from.

A man may if he likes try the experiment of Thoreau, and restrict himself to the merest necessaries of life – so as to see how much labour it really requires to live. Starting from that zero-point he may add to his luxuries and to his labours as he thinks fit. How far he travels along that double line will of course depend upon temperament. Thoreau, as I have said, was a thorough economist. One day he picked up a curiosity and kept it on his shelf for a time; but soon finding that it required dusting he threw it out of the window! It did not pay for its keep. Thoreau preferred leisure to ornaments; other people may prefer ornaments to leisure. There is of course no prejudice – all characters temperaments and idiosyncrasies are welcome and

21

thrice welcome. The only condition is that you must not expect to have the ornaments and the idleness both. If you choose to live in a room full of ornaments no one can make the slightest possible objection, but you must not expect Society (in the form of your maidservant) to dust them for you; unless you do something useful for Society (or your maidservant) in return. (I need not at this time of day say that giving Money is not equivalent to "doing something useful" – unless you have fairly earned the money; then it is.)

Let us have courage. There is ample room within this ideal of Honest Life for all human talent, ingenuity, divergency of thought and temperament. It is not a narrow cramped ideal. How can it be? – for it *alone* contains in it the possibility of human brotherhood. But I warn you: it is *not* compatible with that other ideal of Worldly Gentility. I do not say this lightly. I know what it is for anyone to have to abandon the forms in which he has been brought up; nor do I wish to throw discredit on anyone class, for I know that this ideal permeates more or less the greater part of the nation to-day. But the hour demands absolute fidelity. There is no time now for temporising. England stands on the brink of a crisis in which no wealth, no armaments, no diplomacy will save her – only an awakening of the National Conscience. If this comes she will live – if it comes not?

The canker of effete gentility has eaten into the heart of this nation. Its noble Men and Women are turned into toy ladies and gentlemen; the eternal dignity of (voluntary) Poverty and Simplicity has been forgotten in an unworthy scramble for easy chairs; Justice and Honesty have got themselves melted away into a miowling and watery philanthropy; the rule of honour between master and servant, and servant and master, between debtor and creditor, and buyer and seller, has been turned into a rule of dishonour, concealment, insincere patronage, and sharp bargains; and England lies done to death by her children who should have loved her.

As for you, Working men and Working women of England – in whom now, if anywhere, the hope of England lies – I appeal to you at any rate to cease from this ideal, I appeal to you to cease your part in this Gentility business – to cease respecting people because they wear fine clothes and ornaments, and because they live in grand houses. You know you do these things, or pretend to do them, and to do either is foolish. We have had ducking and forelock-pulling enough. It is time for *you* to assert the dignity of human labour. I do not object to a man saying "sir" to his equal, or to an elder, but I do object to his saying "sir" to broad-cloth or to a balance at the bank. Why don't you say "yes" and have done with it? Remember that you too have to learn the lesson of Honesty. You know that in your heart of hearts you despise this nonsense; you know that when "gentleman's" back is turned you take off his fancy airs, and mimic his incapable importances, or launch out into abuse of one who you think has wronged you. Would it not be worthier, if you have these differences, not to conceal but for the sake a your own self-respect to face them firmly and candidly?

The re-birth of England cannot come without from you, too. On the contrary, whatever is done, you will have to do the greater part of it. You will often have to incur the charge of disrespect; you will have to risk, and to lose situations; you will have to bear ridicule, and -perhaps – arms; Anarchists, Socialists, Communists, you will hear yourselves called. But what would you have? It is no good preaching Democracy with your mouths, if you are going to stand all the while and prop with your shoulders the rotten timbers of Feudalism – of which, riddled as they have been during three centuries by the maggots of Usury, we need say no worse than that it is time they should fall.

I say from this day you must set to work yourselves in word thought and deed to root out this genteel dummy – this hairdresser's Ideal of Humanity – and to establish yourselves (where you stand) upon the broad and sacred ground of human labour. As long as you continue to send men to Parliament because they ride in carriages, or cannot have a meeting without asking a "squire," whom you secretly make fun of, to take the chair, or must have clergymen and baronets patrons of your benefit clubs – so long are you false to your natural instincts, and to your own great destinies.

Be arrogant rather than humble, rash rather than stupidly contented; but, best of all, be firm, helpful towards each other, forgetful of differences, scrupulously honest in yourselves, and charitable even to your enemies, but determined that *nothing* shall move you from the purpose you have set before you – the righteous distribution in society of the fruits of your own and other men's labour, the return to Honesty as the sole possible basis of national life and national safety, and the redemption of England from the curse which rests upon her.

EDWARD CARPENTER

Notes

The pages of TO-DAY are open to the expression of all phases of Socialistic thought. The prominent position which owing to unavoidable circumstances the above article occupies, however, renders it desirable to state that it is not to be taken as a representation of the Editors' views.

1. What this new Ideal of Humanity will be I will not attempt here to foreshadow. Sufficient that *honesty* – the honest human relation – must obviously be essential to it. As the ideal of the Feudal Age was upheld and presented to the world in its great poetry, so the new ideal of the Democratic Age will be upheld and presented to the world in the great poetry of Democracy.

2. An intelligent officer of our own navy having lately, had occasion to inspect one of the naval departments at Washington, tells me that in organisation, alertness, modern information and despatch of business it altogether surpasses our own corresponding Admiralty department, and leaves it far behind!

3. By fine irony called "having an independence."

24

4. The explanation, as far as I can discover, of this mysterious iniquity is as follows. It is a notorious tendency in language, as it progresses, to drop the aspiration. Thus the "h" though common in Latin is extinct .in the derivative Italian and only feebly surviving in French. In English the singular phenomenon presents itself of there being two usages – the "h" being practically extinct among the mass of the people while it is clung to with tenacity by the more or less literary classes (and with exaggerated tenacity by those who ape these classes). The explanation seems to be that the natural progress of language has gone on among the people at large, but has been checked among the lettered classes by the conservative influence of the arts of printing and writing. And that it should be possible for one section of the community thus to slide past the other, and for two usages so to be established, only illustrates the completeness class alienation that exists in this country.

5. James R. Osgood & Co, Boston, 1875.

Social Progress and Individual Effort

The Progress of Society is a subject which occupies much attention now-a-days. We hear the shouts and cries of reformers, and are inclined sometimes to be vexed at their noisy insistence and brandishing of panaceas; but when we come to look into the evils to which they draw our attention – under our very noses as it were – and see how serious they are; when we see the misery, the suffering all around us, and see too how directly in some cases this appears to be traceable to certain institutions, we can hardly be human if we do not make some effort to alter these institutions, and the state of society which goes with them; indeed at times we feel that it is our highest duty to agitate with the noisiest, and insist at all costs that justice should be done, the iniquity swept away.

And yet, on the other hand, when retiring from the heat and noise of conflict, we mount a little in thought and look out over the world, when we realise what indeed every day is becoming more abundantly clear – that Society is the gigantic growth of centuries, moving on in an irresistible and ordered march of its own, with the precision and fatality of an astronomic orb – how absurd seem all our demonstrations! what an idle beating of the air! The huge beast comes on with elephantine tread. The Liberal sits on his head, and the Conservative sits on his tail; but both are borne along whether they will or no, and both are shaken off before long; inevitably, into the dust. One reformer shouts, "This way," and another shouts "That," but the great foot comes down and crushes them both, indifferent, crushes the one who thought he was right and the one who found he was wrong, crushes him who would facilitate its progress and him who would stop it, alike.

I confess that I am continually borne about between these two opposing views. On the one hand is Justice, here and now, which must and *shall* be done. On the other hand is

27

Destiny, indifferent, coming down from eternity, which cannot be altered.

Where does the truth lie? Is there any attainable truth in the matter? Perhaps not. The more I think of it, the more am I persuaded that the true explanations, theories, of the social changes which we see around us, that the forces which produce them, that the purposes which they fulfil, lie deep deep down, unsuspected; that the profoundest hitherto Science (Buckle, Comte, Marx, Spencer, Morgan, and the rest) has hardly done more than touch the skirt of this great subject. The surface indications, currents, are elusive; the apparent purposes very different from the real ones; individuals, institutions, nations, more or less like puppets or pieces in a game; – the hand that moves them altogether unseen, screening itself effectually from observation.

Let me take an illustration. You see a young plant springing out of the ground. You are struck by the eager vital growth of it. What elasticity, energy! how it snatches contributions from the winds and sunlight, and the earth beneath, and rays itself out with hourly fresh adornment! You become interested to know what is the meaning of all this activity. You watch the plant. It unfolds. The leaf-bud breaks and discloses leaves. These, then, are what it has been aiming at.

But in the axils of the leaves are other leaf-buds, and from these more leaves! The young shoot branches and becomes a little tree or bush. The branching and budding go on, a repetition apparently of one formula. Presently, however, a flower-bud appears. Now we see the real object!

Have you then ever carefully examined a flower-bud? Take a rosebud for instance, or better still perhaps, a dahlia. When quite young the buds of these latter are mere green knobs. Cut one across with your pen-knife: you will see a green or whitish mass, apparently without organisation. Cut another open which is more advanced, and you will see traces of structural

28

arrangement, even markings and lines faintly pencilled on its surface, like the markings that shoot thro' freezing water – sketches and outlines of what is to follow. Later, and your bud will disclose a distinct formation; beneath an outer husk or film – transparent in the case of the dahlia – the petals can already be distinguished, marked, though not actually separated from each other. Here they lie in block as it were, conceived yet not shapen, like the statue in the stone, or the thought in the brain of the sculptor. But they are growing momently and expanding. The outermost, or sepals, cohering form a husk, which for a time protects the young bud. But it also confines it. A struggle ensues, a strangulation, and then the husk gives way, falls off or passes into a secondary place, and the bud opens.

And now the petals uncurl and free themselves like living things to the light. But the process is not finished. Each petal expanding shows another beneath, and these younger ones as they open push the older ones outwards, and while these latter are fading there are still new ones appearing in the centre. Envelope after envelope exfoliated – such is the law of life.

At last however within the most intimate petals appears the central galaxy – the group of the sexual organs! And now the flower (the petal-flower) which just before in all its glory of form colour and fragrance seemed to be the culminating expression and purpose of the plant's life, appears as only a means, an introduction, a secondary thing – a mere advertisement and lure to wandering insects. Within it lies the golden circle of the stamens, the magic staff of the pistil, and the precious ark or *seed-vessel*.

Now then we know what it has all been for! But the appearance of the seed-vessel is not the end, it is only a beginning. The flower, the petals, now drop off withered and useless; their work is done. But the seed-vessel begins to swell, to take on structure and form – just as the formless bud did before – there is something at work within. And now it bursts, opens, and falls away. It too is a husk, and no longer of any importance – for within it appear the *seeds*, the objects of all this long toil!

Is the investigation finished? is the process at an end ? – No. Here within this tiny seed lies the promise, the purpose, the vital principle, the law, the inspiration – whatever you like to call it – of this plant's life. Can we find it?

The seed falls to the ground. It swells and takes on form and structure – just as the seed-vessel which enclosed it took on form, and structure before – and as the flower-bud (which enclosed the seed-vessel) did before that – and as the leaf-bud (which enclosed the flower-bud) did before that. The seed falls to the ground; it throws off a husk (always *husks* thrown off!) – and discloses an embryo plant-radicle, plumule and cotyledons-root-shoot, stem, shoot and seed leaves – complete. And the circle begins again.[1]

We are baffled after all! We have followed this extraordinary process, we have seen each stage of the plant-growth appearing first as final, and then only as the envelope of a later stage. We have stripped off, so to speak, husk after husk, in our search for the inner secret of the plant-life – we have got down to the tiny seed. But the seed we have found turns out (like every other stage) to be itself only an envelope – to be thrown away in its turn – what we want lies still deeper down. The plant-life begins again – or rather it never ends – but it does not repeat itself. The young plant is not the same as the parent, and the next generation varies again from this. When the envelopes have been thrown oft a thousand and a hundred thousand times more, a new form will appear; will this be a nearer and more perfect expression than before of that within – lying secret – or otherwise?

To return to Society: I began by noting the contrast, often drawn, between the stern inexorable march of this as a whole, and the equally imperious determination of the individual to interfere with its march – a determination excited by the contemplation of what is called evil, and shapen by an ideal of something better _ arising within him. Think what a commotion there must be within the bud when the petals of a rose are forming! Think what arguments, what divisions, what recriminations, even among the atoms. An organization has to be constructed and completed. It is finished at last, and a petal is formed. It rays itself out in the sun, is beautiful and unimpeachable for a day; then it fades, is pushed off, its work is done-and another from within takes its place.

One social movement succeeds another, the completion of one is the signal for the commencement of the next. Hence there can be no stereotyping: *not* to change is to die – this is the rule of Life; because (and the reason is simple enough) *one* form is not enough to express the secret of life. To express *that* requires an infinite series of forms.

Even a crab cannot get on without changing its shell. It outgrows it. It feels very uncomfortable, pent, sullen and irritable (much as the bud did before the bursting of the husk, or as society does when dead forms and institutions – generally represented by a class in power – confine its growth) – anxious, too, and oppressed with fears. It – the crab – retires under a rock, out of harm's way, and presently crack! the shell scales off, and with quietude and patience from within another more suited to it forms. Yet this latter is not final. It is merely the prelude to another.

The Conservative may be wrong, but the Liberal is just as wrong who considers his reform as ultimate, both are right in so far as they look upon measures as transitory. Beware above all things of utopianism in *measures*! Beware, that is, of regarding any system or scheme of society whatever as final or permanent, whether it be the present, or one to come. The feudal arrangement of society succeeded the clannish and patriarchal, the commercial or competitive system succeeds the feudal, the socialistic succeeds the commercial, and the socialistic is succeeded in its turn by other stages; and each of these includes numerous minor developments. The politician or

31

reformer who regards any of these stages or steps as containing the whole secret and redemption of society commits just the same mistake as the theologian who looks upon any one doctrine as necessary to salvation: He is betrayed into the most frightful harshness, narrow-mindedness, and intolerance – and if he has power will become a tyrant. Just the same danger has to be guarded against by everyone of us in daily life. Who is there who (though his reason may contend against it) does not drop into the habit of regarding some one change in his life and surroundings as containing finally the secret of his happiness, and excited by this immense prospect does not do things which he afterwards regrets, and which end in disappointment? There is a millennium, but it does not belong to any system of society that can be named, nor to any doctrine, belief, circumstance or surrounding of individual life. The secret of the plant-life does not tarry in anyone phase of its growth; it eludes from one phase to another, still lying within and within the latest. It is within the grain of mustard seed; it is so small. Yet it rules and is the purpose of every stage, and is like the little leaven which, invisible in three measures of meal, yet leavened the whole lump.

Of the tendency, of which I have spoken, of social forms to stereotype themselves, Law is the most important and in some sense the most pernicious instance. Social progress is a continual fight against it. Popular customs get hardened into laws. Even thus they soon constitute evils. But in the more complex stages of society, when classes arise, the law-making is generally in the hands of a class, and the laws are hardened (often very hardened) class-practices. These shells have to be thrown off and got rid of at all costs – or rather they will inevitably be thrown off when the growing life of the people underneath forces this liberation. It is a bad sign when a patient 'law-abiding' people submit like sheep to old forms which are really long out-worn. "Where the men and women think lightly of the laws .... there the great city stands," says Walt Whitman.

I remember once meeting with a pamphlet written by an

Italian, whose name I have forgotten, member of a Secularist society, to prove that the Devil was the author of all human progress. Of course that, in his sense, is true. The spirit of opposition to established order, the war against the continuance (as a finality) of any institution or order, however good it may be for the time, is a necessary element of social progress, is a condition of the very life of society. Without this it would die.

Law is a strangulation. Yet while it figures constantly as an evil in social life, it must not therefore be imagined to be bad or without use. On the contrary, its very appearance as an evil is part of its use. It is the husk which protects and strengthens the bud while it confines it. Possibly the very confinement and forcible repression which it exercises is one element in the more rapid organization of the bud within. It is the crab's shell which gives form and stability to the body of the creature, but which has to give way when a more extended form is wanted.

In the present day in modern society the strangulation of the growth of the people is effected by the capitalist class. This class together with its laws and institutions constitutes the husk which has to be thrown off just as itself threw off the husk of the feudal aristocracy in its time. The commercial and capitalist envelope has undoubtedly served to protect and give form to (and even nourish) the growing life of the people. But now its function in that respect is virtually at an end. It appears merely as an obstacle and an evil – and will inevitably be removed, either by a violent disruption or possibly by a gradual absorption into the socialised proletariat beneath.

At all times, and from whatever points of view, it should be borne in mind that laws are made by the people, not the people by the laws. Modern European Society is cumbered by such a huge and complicated overgrowth of law, that the notion actually gets abroad that such machinery is necessary to keep the people in order – that without it the mass of the people would not live an orderly life; whereas all observation of the habits of primitive and savage tribes, destitute of laws and almost destitute of any authoritative institutions – and all observation of the habits of civilised people when freed from law (as in gold-mining and other backwood communities) – show just the reverse. The instinct of man is to an orderly life, the law is but the result and expression of this. As well attribute the organization of a crab to the influence of its shell, as attribute the orderly life of a nation to the action of its laws. Law *has* a purpose and an influence – but the idea that is to preserve order is elusive. All its machinery of police and prisons do not, cannot: do this. At best in this sense it only preserves an order advantageous to a certain class; it is the weapon of a slow and deliberate warfare. It springs from hatred and. rouses opposition, and so has a healthy influence.

Fichte said: "The object of all government is to render government superfluous." And certainly if external authority of any kind has a final purpose it must be to establish and consolidate an internal authority. Whitman adds to his description of "the great city," that it stands "Where outside authority enters always after the precedence of inside authority." When this process is complete, government in the ordinary sense is already "rendered superfluous." Anyhow this external governmental power is obviously self-destructive. It has no permanence or finality about it, but in every period of history appears as a husk or shell preparing the force within which is to reject it.

Thus I have in a very fragmentary and imperfect way called attention to some general conditions of social progress, conditions by which the growth of Society is probably comparable with the growth of a plant or an animal or an astronomic organism, subject to laws and an order of its own, in face of which the individual would at first sight appear to count as nothing. But there is, as usual, a counter-truth which must not be overlooked. If Society moves by an ordered and irresistible march of its own, so also – as a part of Society, and beyond that as a part of Nature – does the individual. In his right place the individual is also irresistible.

34

Now then, when you have seized your life-inspiration, your absolute determination, *you* also are irresistible, the whole weight of this vast force is behind you. Huge as the institutions of Society are, vast as is the sweep of its traditions and customs, yet in face of it all, the word "I will" is not out of place.

Let us take the law of the competitive struggle for existence – which has been looked upon by political economists (perhaps with some justice) as the base of social life. It is often pointed out that this law of competition rules throughout the animal and vegetable kingdoms as well as through the region of human society, and therefore, it is said, being evidently a universal law of Nature, it is useless and hopeless to expect that society can ever be founded on any other basis. Yet I say that granting this assumption – and in reality the same illusion underlies the application of the word "law" here, as we saw before in its social application – granting I say that competition has hitherto been the universal law, the last word, of Nature, still if only one man should stand up and say, "It shall be so no more," – if he should say, "It is not the last word of my nature, and my acts and life declare that it is not," then that so-called law would be at an end. He being a part of Nature has as much right to speak as any other part, and as in the elementary law of hydrostatics a slender column of water can balance (being at the same height) against an ocean – so his Will (if he understand it aright) can balance all that can be arrayed against him. If only one man – with regard to social matters – speaking from the bottom of his heart says "This shall not be: behold something better;" his word is stronger than all institutions, all traditions. And why? – because the bottom of his heart is also that of Society, of Man. Within himself, in quiet, he has beheld the secret, he has seen a fresh crown of petals, a golden circle of stamens, folded and slumbering in the bud. Man forms society, its laws and institutions, and Man can re-form them. Somewhere within yourself be assured, the secret of that authority lies.

The fatal words spoken by individuals – the words of

progress – are provoked by what is called *evil*. Every human institution is good in its time, and then becomes evil – yet it may be doubted whether it is really evil in itself, but rather because if it remained it would hinder the next step. Each petal is pushed out by the next one. A new growth of the moral sense takes place first within the individual – and this gives birth to a new ideal, something to love better than anything seen before. Then in the light of this new love, this more perfect desire, what has gone before and the actually existing things appear wizened and *false* (i.e., ready to *fall* – like the petals). They become something to hate, they are evil; and the perception of evil is already the promise of something better.

Do not be misled so as to suppose that science and the intellect are or can be the sources of social progress or change. It is the moral births and outgrowths that originate, science and the intellect only give form to these. It is a common notion and one apparently gaining ground that science may as it were take Society by the hand and become its high priest and guide to a glorious kingdom. And this to a certain extent is true. Science may become high-priest, but the result of its priestly offices will entirely depend on what kind of deity it represents – what kind of god Society worships. Science will doubtless become its guide, but whither it leads Society will entirely depend on whither Society desires to be led. If Society worships a god of selfish curiosity the holy rites and priesthood of science will consist in vivisection and the torture of the loving animals; if society believes above all things in material results, and desires material gains, science will before long provide these things – it will surround men with machinery and machine-made products, it will whirl them about (behind steam-kettles as Mr. Ruskin says) from one end of the world to the other, it will lap them in every luxury and debility, and give them fifty thousand toys to play with where before they had only one – but through all the whistling of the kettles and the rattling of the toys it will not make the still small voice of God sound any nearer: If Society, in short, worships the devil, science will lead it to the devil; and if Society worships God science will open up, and clear away much that encumbered the path to God. (And here I use these terms as lawyers say "without prejudice"). No mere scientific adjustments will bring about the millennium. Granted that the problem is Happiness, there must be certain moral elements in the mass of mankind before they will even *desire* that kind of happiness which is attainable, let alone their capacity of reaching it – when these moral elements are present the intellectual or scientific solution of the problem will be soon found, without them there will not really be any serious attempt made to find it. That is – as I said at the head of this paragraph- science and the intellect are not, and never can be, the sources of social progress and change. It is the moral births and outgrowths that originate; the intellect stands in a secondary place as the tool and instrument of the moral faculty.

The commercial and competitive state of society indicates to my mind an upheaval from the feudal of a new (and perhaps grander) sentiment of human right and dignity. Arising simultaneously with Protestantism it meant – they both meant – individualism, the assertion of man's worth and dignity as man, and as against any feudal lordship or priestly hierarchy. It was an outburst of feeling first. It was the sense of equality spreading. It took the form of individualism – the equality of rights – protestantism in religion, competition in commerce. It resulted in the social emancipation of a large class, the *bourgeoisie*. Feudalism, now dwindled to a husk, was thrown off; and for a time the glory, the life of society was in the new order.

But to-day a wider morality, or at least a fresh impulse, asserts itself. Competition in setting itself up as the symbol of human equality, was (like all earthly representations of what is divine) only an imperfect symbol. It had the elements of mortality and dissolution in it. For while it destroyed the privilege of rank and emancipated a huge class, it ended after all by enslaving another class and creating the privilege of wealth. Competition in fact represented a portion of human equality but not the whole; insisting on individual rights all round, it overlooked the law of charity, turned sour with the acid of selfishness, and became as to-day the gospel of "the devil take the hindmost." Arising glorious as the representative of human equality and the opponent of iniquity in high places, it has ended by denying the very source from whence it sprung. It passes by, and like Moses in the rock we now behold the back parts of our divinity!

Competition is doomed. Once a good, it has now become an evil. But simultaneously (and probably as part of the same process) springs up, as I say, a new morality. Everywhere to-day signs of this may be seen, felt. It is *felt* that the relation which systematically allows the weaker to go to the wall is not *human*. Individualism, the mere separate pursuit, each of his own good, on the basis of equality, does not satisfy the heart. The right (undoubted though it may be) to take advantage of another's weakness or inferiority, does not please us any longer. Science and the intellect have nothing to say to this, for or against, – they can merely stand and look on – arguments may be brought on both sides. What I say is that as a fact a change is taking place in the general sentiment in this matter; some deeper feeling of human solidarity, brotherliness, charity, some more genuine and substantial apprehension of the meaning of the word equality, is arising – some broader and more determined sense of justice. Though making itself felt as yet only here and there, still there are indications that this new sentiment is spreading; and if it becomes anything like general, then inevitably (I say) it will bring a new state of society with it – will be in fact such new state of society.

Some years ago at Brighton I met with William Smith, the author of "Thorndale" and other works – a man who had thought much about society and human life. He was then quite an invalid, and indeed died only a week or two later. Talking one day about the current political Economy he said: "They assume self-interest as the one guiding principle of human nature and so make it the basis of their science" – "but," he added, "even if it is so now it may not always be so, and that would entirely re-model their science." I do not know whether he was aware that even then a new school of political economy was in existence, the school of Marx, Engels, Lassalle, and others – founded really on just this new basis, taking as its point of departure a stricter sense of justice and a new conception of human right and equality. At any rate, whether aware or not, I contend that this dying man – even if he had been alone in the world in his aspiration – feeling within himself a deeper, more intimate, principle of action than that expressed in the existing state of society, might have been confident that at some time or other – if not immediately – it would come to the surface and find its due interpretation and translation in a new order of things. And I contend that whoever to-day feels in himself that there is a better standard of life than the higgling of the market, and a juster scale of wages than "what A. or B. will take," and a more important question in any undertaking than "how much per cent. it will pay" -contains or conceals *in himself* the germs of a new social order.

Socialism, if that is to be the name of the next wave of social life, springs from and demands as its basis a new sentiment of humanity, a higher morality. That is the essential part of it. A science it is, but only secondarily; for we must remember that as, the *bourgeois* political economy sprang from certain moral data, so the socialist political economy implies other moral data. Both are irrefragable on their own axioms. And when these axioms in course of time change again (as they infallibly will) another science of political economy, again irrefragable, will spring up, and socialist political economy will be false.

The morality being the essential part of the movement, it is important to keep that in view. If Socialism, as Mr. Matthew Arnold has pointed out, means merely a change of society without a change of its heart – if it merely means that those who grabbed, all the good things before shall be displaced, and that those who, were grabbed from shall now grab in their turn – it amounts to nothing, and is not in effect a change at all, except quite upon the surface. If it is to be a substantial movement, it must mean a changed ideal, a changed conception of daily life; it must mean some better conception of human dignity – such as shall scorn to claim anything for its own which has not been duly earned, and such as shall not find itself degraded by the doing of any work, however menial, which is useful to society; it must mean simplicity of life, defence of the weak, courage of one's own convictions, charity of the faults and failings of others. These things first, and a larger slice of pudding all round afterwards!

How can such morality be spread? – How does a plant grow?- It grows. There is some contagion of influence in these matters. Knowledge can be taught directly; but a new ideal, a new sentiment of life, can only pass by some indirect influence from one to another. Yet it does pass. There is no need to talk – perhaps the less said in any case about these matters the better – but if you have such new ideal within you, it is I believe your clearest duty, as well as your best interest, to act it out in your own life at all apparent costs. Then we must not forget that a wise order of society once established (by the strenuous action of a few) reacts on its members. To a certain extent it is true, perhaps, that men and women can be *grown* – like cabbages. And this is a case of the indirect influence of the strenuous few upon the many.

Thus – in this matter of society's change and progress – (though I feel that the subject as a whole is far too deep for me) – I do think that the birth of new moral conceptions in the individual is at least a very important factor. It may be in one individual of in a hundred thousand. As a rule probably when one man feels any such impulse strongly, the hundred thousand are nearer to him than he suspects. (When one leaf, or petal, or stamen begins to form on a tree, or one plant begins to push its way above the ground in spring, there are hundreds of thousands all around just ready to form.) Anyhow, whether he is alone or not, the new moral birth is sacred – as sacred as the child within the mother's womb – it is a kind of blasphemy against the holy ghost to conceal it. And when I use the word "moral" here – or anywhere above – I do not, I hope, mean that dull stupid pinch-lipped conventionality of negations which often goes under that name. The deep-lying ineradicable desires, fountains of human action, the life-long aspirations, the lightning-like revelations of right and justice, the treasured hidden ideals, born in flame and in darkness, in joy and sorrow, in tears and in triumph, within the heart – are as a rule anything but conventional. They may be, and often are, thought immoral. I don't care, they are sacred just the same. If they underlie a man's life, and are nearest to himself – they will underlie humanity. "To your own self be true ...."

Anyhow courage is better than conventionality: take your stand and let the world come round to you. Do not think you are right and everybody else wrong. If you think you are wrong then you may be right; but if you think you are right then you are certainly wrong. Your deepest highest moral conceptions are only for a time. They have to give place. They are the envelopes of Freedom – that eternal Freedom which cannot be represented – that peace which passes understanding. Somewhere here is the invisible vital principle, the seed within the seed. It may be held but not thought, felt but not represented – except by Life and History. Every individual so far as he touches this stands at the source of social progress – behind the screen on which the phantasmagoria play.

EDWARD CARPENTER

Notes

1. Though not really a circle – any more than the paths of the planets are really ellipses.

Does it Pay?

Having lately embarked in an agricultural enterprise on a small scale, I confess I was somewhat disconcerted, if not actually annoyed, by the persistency with which – from the very outset, and when I had been only two or three months at work – I was met by the question at the head of this paper. Not only sisters, cousins, and aunts, but relations much more remote, and mere acquaintances, at the very first suggestion that I was engaged in trade, always plumped out with the query, Does it pay? And this struck me the more because in the innocence of my heart I fear I had not sufficiently realised the importance of this point. At any rate it had seemed to me that there *might* be other considerations of comparable weight. But I soon found out my mistake; for none of my well-to-do friends asked whether the work I was doing was wanted, or whether it would be useful to the community, or a means of healthy life to those engaged in it, or whether it was *honest* and of a kind that could be carried on without interior defilement; or even (except one or two) whether I liked it, but always: does it pay? I say my well-to-do friends, because I couldn't help remarking that while the workers generally ask me such questions, as whether the soil was good, or adapted to the purpose, the crops fine, the water abundant, & c., it was always the rich who asked the distinctively commercial question – a professional question as it appeared to me, and which marked them as a class, and their modes of thought. Not that I have any quarrel with them for asking it, because the question is undoubtedly, in some sense, a very important one, and one which has to be asked; rather I ought to feel grateful and indebted, because it forced me to think about a matter that I had not properly considered before.

What then did it mean? What was the exact sense of the expression, does it pay? as here used? On enquiring I found it came to this: "When you have subtracted from your gross receipts all expenses for wages of labour, materials, & c., is there a balance equivalent to four or five per cent. on your outlay of capital? If *yes,* it pays; if no, it doesn't." Clearly if the thing came up to this standard or surpassed it, it was worthy of attention; if it didn't it would be dismissed as unimportant and soon be dropped and abandoned. This was clear and definite, and at first I felt greatly relieved to have arrived at so solid a conclusion. But after a time, and carrying on the enterprise farther, I am sorry to say that my ideas (for they have a great tendency that way) again began to get misty, and I could not feel sure that I had arrived at any certain principle of action.

My difficulty was that I began to feel that even supposing the concern only brought me in *one* per cent., it was quite as likely as not that I should still stick to it. For I thought that if I was happy in the life, and those working with me were well-content too, and if there were children growing up on the place under tolerably decent and healthy conditions, and if we were cultivating genuine and useful products, cabbages land apples or what not – that it might really pay me better to get one per cent. for that result, even if it involved living quite simply and inexpensively, than ten per cent. with jangling and wrangling, over-worked and sad faces round me, and dirty and deceptive stuff produced; and that if I could afford it I might even think it worth while to *pay* to keep the first state going, rather than be paid for the second.

I knew it was very foolish of me to think so, and bad Political Economy, and I was heartily ashamed of myself, but still I couldn't help it. I knew the P.E.'s would say that if I disregarded the interest on my capital I should only be disturbing natural adjustments, that my five per cent. was an index of what was wanted, a kind of providential arrangement harmonising my interest (literally) with that of the mass of mankind, and that if I was getting only one per cent. while others were sending in the same stuff from France and getting ten per cent., it was clear that I was wasting labour by trying to do here what could be done so much more profitably somewhere else, and that I ought to give way. This was what I knew they would say; but then from my own little experience I readily saw that the ten per cent. profit might mean no superior advantage of labour in that part, but merely superior grinding and oppression of the labourer by the employer, superior disadvantage of the labourer in fact; and that if I gave way in its favour, I should only be encouraging the extortion system. I should be playing into the hands of some nefarious taskmaster in another part of the industrial world, and by increasing his profits should perhaps encourage others, still more unscrupulous, to undersell him, which of course they would do by further exactions from the worker; and so on and on. I saw too that if I abandoned my enterprise, I should have to discharge my workpeople, with great chance of their getting no fresh employment, and to them I had foolishly become quite attached; which was another serious trouble, but I could not help it.

And so in all this confusion of mind, and feeling quite certain that I could not understand all the complexities of the science of Political Economy myself, and having a lurking suspicion that even the most able professors were in the dark about some points, I began to wonder if the most sensible and obvious thing to do were not just to try and keep at least one little spot of earth clean: actually to try and produce clean and unadulterated food, to encourage honest work, to cultivate decent and healthful conditions for the workers, arid useful products for the public and to maintain this state of affairs as long as I was able, taking my chance of the pecuniary result to myself. It would not be much, but it would be something, just a little glimmer as it were in the darkness; but if others did the same, the illumination would increase, and after a time perhaps we should all be able to see our way better.

I knew that this method of procedure would not be "scientific" – that it would be beginning at the wrong end for that – but then as I have said I felt in despair about my ever being clever enough really to understand the science – and as, to half-knowledge, that might be more misleading than none. It was like the advice in the Bible: "Seek ye first the kingdom of

God and his righteousness, and all these things shall be added unto you," obviously irrational and absurd, and any argument would expose the fallacy of it, and yet I felt inclined to adopt it.

For when on the other hand I tried to make a start along the ordinary lines, I found myself from the outset in a hopeless bog! I could not, for the life of me, tell *how much* I ought to take as interest, and how much I ought to give in wages – the increase of the former evidently depending on the smallness of the latter. If I adopted just the current rate of wages, there was nothing in that, for I knew that they represented a mere balance of extortion on the one hand, and despair on the other, and how could I take that as my principle of action? If I gave more than the current rate I should very likely get no interest at all, and so be consigned to perdition by all my well-to-do friends, including the Professors of Political Economy; while if I gave less, I should certainly go to hell in my own eyes. And though I pondered over this dilemma, or rather trilemma, till I was sick of it, I never could see my way out of it.

And then I reflected that even if I was lucky enough to pitch on some principle of wage-payment which would leave a nice little balance of Interest – it was quite doubtful, whether I should feel any right to appropriate such balance to my own use. That also was a great trouble. For I could not help seeing that after taking my proportional payment for my labours in the concern, and some small remuneration for my care of superintendencies, if I then appropriated a considerable interest on the Capital laid out, I should without any extra work be much better off than my coadjutors. And though the P.E.'s assured me this was all right, and kind of providential, I had serious qualms, which, do what I would, I could not shake off. I felt keenly that what I should then be taking, would only be so much subtracted from the wages of these others, and that the knowledge of this would disturb the straightforward relation between us, and I should no longer be able to look them in the face.

I could not help seeing too that it was by means of this *general system of the appropriation of balances* that a very curious phenomenon was kept up – an enormous class, to wit, living in idleness and luxury, they and their children and their children's children, till they became quite incapable of doing anything for themselves or even of thinking rightly about most things – tormented with incurable *ennui,* and general imbecility and futility; all art and literature, which were the appendage of this class, being affected by a kind of St. Vitus' dance; and the whole thing breaking out finally for want of any other occupation into a cuff and collar cult, called respectability.

And then I began to see more clearly the meaning of the question (asked by this class) – does *it pay?* – *i.e.,* Can we continue drawing from the people nourishment enough to keep our St. Vitus' dance going? I thought I saw a vision of poor convulsed creatures, decked out in strange finery, in continual antic dance peering in each other's faces, with eager questioning as to whether the state of profits would allow the same doleful occupation to go on for ever. And all the more eager I saw them on account of the dim wandering consciousness they had that the whole thing was not natural and right, and the presentiment that it could not last very long. And then I saw a vision of the new society in which the appropriation of balances was not the whole object of life; but things were produced primarily for the use and benefit of those who should consume them. It was actually thought that it *paid better* to work on that principle; and strangely enough, the kingdom of heaven was at the centre of that society – and the "other things" were added unto it. But there was no respectability there, for the balances that could be privately appropriated were not large enough even to buy starch with, and a great many people actually went without collars.

And so I saw that the eager question (in the particular sense on which it had been asked me) was in fact a symptom of the decay of the old Society – a kind of dying grin and death-rattle of respectability – and that a new order, a new life, was already preparing beneath the old, in which there would be no need for it to be asked; or if asked, then in which it should be asked in a new sense.

EDWARD CARPENTER.

Trade

I suppose the peculiar character of our commercial age – its excellencies and its defects – can be as well studied in the market as anywhere. The first time I stood behind my own goods, and spread out peas and potatoes, roses and raspberries, of my own growing, to the eye of the customer, I felt that I was passing behind a veil, many things were becoming clear! I had often been in the market as a buyer, and had, I am sorry to say, been accustomed to look upon the tradesman as a personification of artful wickedness – one who combined with his fellows to defraud the public and to take advantage of its innocence. But now I had passed myself into that inner circle, and with what a different eye did I regard the situation! It seemed to me now that it was the public which was at fault. I seemed to see at a glance the original sinfulness of its disposition. How out of its naughty old heart it suspected you always and always of putting the bad stuff at the bottom of the basket; how it would beat you down shamelessly, if it could, to prices below the zero of any possible remuneration to the grower; how it would handle fruit and flowers till all the delicate bloom was gone, and then pass by with a scoff – (things, all of which I had *once* done myself); and how, instead of desiring to do as it would be done by, its one guiding fear, overruling all lesser sentiments of honesty and humanity, was lest it should be *done* as it would desire to *do*. Hitherto I had looked upon cheap goods as a blessing, but now I saw, or seemed to see, that they meant general ruin. For cheap goods mean low wages, scarcity of money; meant hungry faces going by, and hands fingering half-pence, long and anxiously, before parting with them; meant slow sales and poor returns to the trader. While scarcity and high prices seemed no longer the unmixed evil I had supposed, for likely as not they were the indication of a brisk demand, full pockets, and general prosperity.

Thus my change of position, from the front to the back of a stall, wrought at once a considerable alteration in my views of some social matters. I took a new view of the world. My axiom was changed, and consequently a lot of theorems which I had thought were well established fell to pieces, and became sadly invalid. I found the inner circle of the market a vantage ground, too, for the study of human nature. Here the buyers are the performers. They occupy the arena, and are exposed to a considerable criticism from behind the stalls. The seller, on the other hand, is comparatively unobserved. The buyer eyes the strawberries, old bird though he be he cannot entirely hide the gleam of his satisfaction at their appearance.

"How much?" he asks carelessly. "Five shillings a peck" is your equally careless reply. You know the fruit is first rate. You know also that he knows it; and he probably knows that you know that he knows it. "Eh, what are you talking about?" is his answer, and in assumed disgust he goes off down the market. Presently you see him coming back again; he has been all round; but as he goes by, crafty he scarce glances at the coveted stuff. Not till he has got to a safe distance, and to a spot where he thinks he may stand unobserved does he turn again and measure it over with his eye. Now, then, you are satisfied; you know that you are safe about those strawberries, and you may give your attention to the sale of other things. You know also (what is very important) that there is no better fruit of the same kind, and at the same price in the market. Great is your triumph when, after some delay, your customer returns (as he infallibly will do) and you are able to tell him that the produce in question is all sold, or that the *price has risen*.

On the whole though the maxims of business are not too lofty, the thorough business people are the most satisfactory to deal with. They waste no time in whatever higgling is necessary, they know a little of both sides of the question, and are inclined to treat you as a reasonable creature, and are prompt and methodical. This carefully-dressed somewhat stout matron with curls, looks a little old-fashioned, but she has a shrewd eye and a kindly heart; she keeps a shop and knows pretty well how prices stand both for buyer and seller; is pleasant to deal with, and not disinclined to put her custom on a friendly and permanent footing. Here comes a man who considers himself quite the boss of the market – brisk and business-like, with extensive watch-chain, and elegant flower in his button-hole; he is a large dealer and acts as if he were doing you the honour to be your customer. Nevertheless, one can get on with him; but this abominable Irishwoman who always turns up, talking nineteen to the dozen, and wanting to beg everything at shameless prices, and then when the bargain is concluded, asking for this to be thrown in and that to be thrown in, is really more than I can bear. Then there is an unpleasant-looking ferret-eyed man who always suspects me of having put the best potatoes at the top; I do not like him, and feel no satisfaction in selling anything to him. But this little man in carefully-brushed great-coat and tall hat, is really a pleasure to deal with. He is a retail customer, and is quite a Pickwickian study, has an immense red nose, which must occupy nearly all his field of view, yet of drinking I am sure he is blameless, so affable and scrupulous is he; and when he buys a peck of peas I feel certain he will take them home and shell them sitting by his wife's side. There is the working wife too, who wants a nice cauliflower for the Sunday dinner, but ultimately decides on a cabbage on account of the price; and the young man who wants a button-hole for his girl. He chooses the most lovely of the rose-buds, but pauses when he hears what he has to pay (for the season is advanced) – he retires for a moment, and then comes forward like a man and secures his prize.

Those who know something about the labour of production – either in the trade in question or in some other trade – are often most reasonable to deal with. They can sympathise to some extent with you. I find that the "lady" or "gentleman " is often inclined to beat one down, or refuse a rational price out of mere ignorance – not knowing what they ought to give, they assume that whatever you ask must be an imposition. And of course, on the other hand, they often are imposed upon by the unscrupulous. I confess that I have been inclined to take this latter part myself. There is a widespread impression among the "people" that the wealthy class are lawful prey. Perhaps they are – it might be difficult to decide one way or the other – but anyhow the gap, or the want of sympathetic relation, between the two parties, makes their dealings with one another unsatisfactory.

With regard to the higgling of the prices, and the law of supply and demand, it is interesting to see how rapidly you feel from your own particular stand the general state of the market, how organically you seem to form a part of it. You drive over the hills by sunrise, plunging down through the clear light and by the dewy hedgerows into the still quiet streets of the great city; you find yourself in a bustling, noisy market, you open out your goods, take a cursory glance at the quantity of stuff in of various kinds, and mentally fix on the probable prices. The stream of customers flows by. "How much?? "how much?? how much?? Different as are the characters of the individuals comprising the crowd, various as are their little dodges and artifices, the total effect is soon averaged. As you reply to each, expressions of disgust or satisfaction involuntarily pass over their faces, and in a few minutes you know quite certainly how you stand – your little gland which is washed by the general circulation soon gets congested with traffic or left high and dry – and your relation to the rest of the market is established.

I should be inclined to think that, unless it be the petroleum market, there is no market which fluctuates so rapidly as the vegetable and fruit market. Frosts spoil tons of cauliflowers, rain nine acres of strawberries; a few fine days in spring will cause parsley to fall from three shillings a pound to as many pence. From week to week in some articles it is impossible to tell what the price will be. You bring in a load of fine celery roots and the market is glutted with celery, there are tons and tons in, and it is as good as given away to the street-hawkers; another day it is just as scarce – everyone has held back – and poor stuff fetches a good price. Even from hour to hour the variations are remarkable, some things will run out and run up, other things will remain abundant to the very close of the market, and have to be sold at last for a mere song Quite a class of small traders and hawkers lie in wait for last casualty, and make their living by buying what else would be shot up on the manure heap. Still, though competition thus holds sway, and can, so to speak, be felt in operation, yet it is difficult to reduce the law of supply and demand to anything like an absolute generalisation, or to make it practically applicable except in the roughest way. Custom which is a force antagonistic to competition, and which has at one time undoubtedly been the main determinate of prices, which is certainly one of the strongest forces of human nature, and which will have to be reckoned with in any forecast of the future adjustments of commerce, custom acts strongly to-day in the markets, even in the very teeth of the fierce competition that exists. Customary prices model competition prices; for very shame large numbers of people will not buy and will not sell at rates which they consider abnormal; a latent sense of honour withholds them; the tendency of buyers and sellers to establish permanent and friendly dealings with each other, a tendency which I an inclined to think lies at the base of all exchange, and which has created, I suppose, the word "customer" is still quite strongly traceable, the effort of the human to assert itself as against the merely mechanical being yet not quite extinct. Then there are nameless preferences – as of individuals for particular varieties of goods – or of classes of buyers for particular classes of sellers; nameless habits, traditions, predilections or prejudices, and this in every trade, anomalies which competition ought to level down but somehow it does not. Undoubtedly the tendency to a mechanical level may be said to exist, but that level or anything like a level is ever over reached is quite a different thing. It is like a basin of water being carried about in the hand, the water should go horizontal, but the disturbances arising from the human side effectually prevent this being realised. Thus competition when one becomes practically acquainted with it, when one comes to feel its operation, appears somewhat as a force acting on the human – acting I would almost say to degrade or warp the human within one. It does not appear as an isolated and self-sufficient law of exchange, but just as one factor in the problem, a factor which, if it had everything its own way, would speedily reduce commerce to a mere mechanical function devoid of all humanity. This, however, is a result which is impossible, because no function of human nature can be separated from humanity and made purely mechanical without *ipso facto* withering away and dying. And thus we have the alternative that commerce must either go on in its present direction and perish, or live by retiring to human relationship as its basis.

"I have tried trade," says Thoreau, "but I found it would take ten years to get under-way in that, and that then I should probably be on my way to the devil." And again he says, "Trade curses everything it handles." I myself have never met any one who seriously maintained that success in trade was in the long run compatible with honesty. These charges however may not be so damnatory as they appear, for after all perhaps it does not matter so much whether trade can be carried on honestly or not, as whether you *try* to carry it on honestly. The use of trade, as perhaps of every other pursuit, is mainly to test your probity and I should say that for that purpose it is excellently adapted. The strains it puts upon you are severe. Quite decisively you cannot worship *both* God and Mammon in it. If however folks generally tried to carry on trade honestly, very probably a new form of exchange would soon develop itself which would allow of honesty being realised.

I do not think that the difficulty about trade lies chiefly in the market, but rather in its influence, indirectly, on production. The market, on the whole, with all its chicanery, its worship of cuteness, its besting and bluffing, is an intensely human institution, the very fact that you are forced into contact with such a number of your fellow-creatures has a redeeming influence. And some useful qualities, such as alertness, forethought, patience and judgment, have undoubtedly been developed by it. But its influence on production is to my mind deadly and numbing. To feel that you are working for the market kills all interest in your work.

I feel this quite decisively myself. When I am working for use, when I am hoeing potatoes and thinking of them only as food – thinking how somebody will eat them at any rate – and studying how to grow them best for that purpose, then I am assured good before me, which no one can take away. Whatever their price, these potatoes will feed the same number of human beings. I feel calm and contentful, and can take pleasure in my work. But when I am working for the market, when the profit and the gain which I am to derive from sale of my potatoes is the main object before me – when I am considering all along whether each thrust of the hoe will pay, whether I had not better scamp this or hurry over that in view of the falling prices, when I see that the whole end and purpose of my labour is involved in doubt owing to trade fluctuations which I cannot possibly foresee – then – (how can it be otherwise?) I am miserable and feverish, grudging every stroke of the tool in my hand, each effort of the muscles, tossed about by uncertainty, wavering in my plans, and devoid of that good heart which alone is the basis of all good work. Certainly I may be, shall be, longer over my work in the first case than in the second; but I shall produce better stuff – and if I enjoy my work I shall not mind an hour additional at it, but if I hate it, all the time spent on it is lost. Business conducted on the latter principal may be tolerable, while the prospect of winning draws one on, and before the gambling pleasure has palled, but after that, no! The whole of production to-day is vitiated by the fact that it is production for gain, for profit. There is no assured good in it, no certain advantage or enjoyment in the work – success depends on conditions which are beyond the control of the worker or employer. But it is not wise for any one to let success depend on things which are beyond his control. The evil principle searches down and affects the lowermost grades of industry, and there is hardly a man now-a-days to be found who is said to be happy in his work. Yet if production were for use, success would be within the reach of everybody. No man, if he only worked for five minutes, need fear that his work will be lost by a fluctuation of the market. No fluctuation the market will spoil the knife-edge that I have been grinding nor any change in the price of turnips make these that I am singling less useful for food. My work is secure when have done it well, and its result is secure – I can whistle and sing at my ease.

Trade is against nature, it is in the long run against human nature, as long as "What can I get?" is its motto. The true nature of man is to give, like the sun; his getting must be subordinate to that. When giving, his thoughts are on others and he is "free;" when getting, his thoughts are on himself, he is anxious, therefore, and miserable. As long as Trade takes "What can I get?" for its axiom, anxiety and misery will characterise all its work as they do to-day.

EDWARD CARPENTER

Defence of Criminals – Criticism of Immorality I

A criminal is literally a person accused – accused, and in the modern sense of the word convicted, of being harmful to society. But is he there in the dock, the patch-coated brawler or burglar, really harmful to society? is he more harmful than the mild old gentleman in the wig who pronounces sentence upon him? That is the question. Certainly he has infringed the law: and the law is in a sense the consolidated public opinion of society: but if no one were to break the law public opinion would ossify, and society would die. As a matter of fact society keeps changing its opinion. How then are we to know when it is right and when it is wrong? The Outcast of one age is the Hero of another. In execration they nailed Roger Bacon's manuscripts out in the sun and rain, to rot crucified upon planks – his bones lie in an unknown and unhonoured grave – yet to-day he is regarded as a pioneer of human thought. The hated Christian holding his ill-famed love-feasts in the darkness of the catacombs has climbed on to the throne of S. Peter and the world. The Jew money-lender whom Front-de-Boeuf could torture with impunity is become a Rothschild – guest of princes and instigator of commercial wars; and Shylock is now a highly respectable Railway Bondholder. And the Accepted of one age is the Criminal of the next. All the glories of Alexander do not condone in our eyes for his cruelty in crucifying the brave defenders of Tyre by thousands along the sea-shore; and if Solomon with his thousand wives and concubines were to appear in London to-morrow, even our most frivolous circles would be shocked, and Brigham Young by contrast seem a domestic model. The judge pronounces sentence on the prisoner now, but society in its turn and in the lapse of years pronounces sentence on the judge. It holds in its hand a new canon, a new code of morals, and consigns its former representative and the law which he administered to a limbo of contempt.

It seems as if Society, as it progresses from point to point, forms ideals – just as the individual does. At any moment each person, consciously or unconsciously, has an ideal in his mind toward which he is working (hence the importance of literature). Similarly Society has an ideal in its mind. These ideals are tangents or vanishing points of the direction in which Society is moving at the time. It does not reach its ideal, but it goes in that direction – then, after a time, the direction of its movement changes, and it has a new ideal.

When the ideal of Society is material gain or possession, as it is largely to-day, the object of its special condemnation is the thief – not the rich thief, for he is already in possession and therefore respectable, but the poor thief. There is nothing to show that the poor thief is really more immoral or unsocial than the respectable money-grubber; but it is very clear that the money-grubber has been floating with the great current of Society, while the poor man has been swimming against it, and so has been worsted. Or when, as to-day, Society rests on private property in land, its counter-ideal is the poacher. If you go in the company of the county squirearchy and listen to the after-dinner talk you will soon think the poacher a combination of all human and diabolic vices; yet I have known a good many poachers, and either have been very lucky in my specimens or singularly prejudiced in their favour, for I have always found them very good fellows – but with just this one blemish that they invariably regard a landlord as an emissary of the evil one! The poacher is as much in the right, probably, as the landlord, but he is not right for the time. He is asserting a right (and an instinct) belonging to a past time – when for hunting purposes all land was held in common – or to a time in the future when such or similar rights shall be restored. Caesar says of the Suevi that they tilled the ground in common, and had no private lands, and there is abundant evidence that all early human communities before they entered on the stage of modern civilisation were communistic in character. Some of the Pacific Islanders to-day are in the same condition. In those times private property was theft. Obviously the man who attempted to retain for himself land or goods, or who fenced off a portion of the common ground and – like the modern landlord – would allow no one to till it who did not pay him a tax – was a criminal of the deepest dye. Nevertheless the criminals pushed their way to the front, and have become the respectables of modern society. And it is quite probable that in like manner the criminals of to-day will push to the front and become the respectables of a later age.

The ascetic and monastic ideal of early Christian and mediaeval ages is now regarded as foolish, if not wicked; and poverty, which in many times and places has been held in honour as the only garb of honesty, is condemned as criminal and indecent. Nomadism – if accompanied by poverty – is criminal in modern society. To-day the gipsy and the tramp are hunted down. To have no settled habitation, or worse still (like him of Nazareth) no place to lay your head, are suspicious matters. We close even our outhouses and barns against the son of man, and so to us the son of man comes not. And yet – at one time and in one stage of human progress – the nomadic state is the rule; and the settler is then the criminal. His crops are fired and his cattle driven off. What right has he to lay a limit to the hunting grounds, or to spoil the wild free life of the plains with his dirty agriculture?

As to the marriage relation and its attendant moralities, the forms are numerous and notorious enough. Public opinion seems to have varied through all phases and ideals, and yet there is no indication of finality. Late investigations show that at an early period in all human societies the marriage tie is very promiscuous – the relation of brother and sister in this respect being rather the rule than the exception; in the present day such a bond as the last-mentioned would be considered inhuman and monstrous.[1] Polyandry prevails among one people or at one time, polygamy prevails among another people or at another time. In Central Africa to-day the chief offers you his wife as a mark of hospitality, in India the native Prince keeps her hidden, even from his most intimate guest. Among the Japanese, public opinion holds young women – even of good birth – singularly free in their intercourse with men, *till they are married*; at Paris they are free after. In the Greek and Roman antiquity marriage seems with some brilliant exceptions to have been a prosaic affair – mostly a matter of convenience and housekeeping – the woman an underling – little of the ideal attaching to the relationship of man and wife. The romance of love went elsewhere. The better class of free women or Hetaerae were those who gave a spiritual charm to the passion. They were an educated and recognised body, and possibly in their best times exercised a healthy and discriminating influence upon the male youth. The respectful treatment of Theodota by Socrates, and the advice which he gives her, concerning her lovers: to keep the insolent from her door, and to rejoice greatly when the accepted succeed in anything honourable, indicates this. That their influence was at times immense the mere name of Aspasia is sufficient to show; and if Plato in the Symposium reports correctly the words of Diotima, her teaching on the subject of human and divine love was probably the noblest and profoundest that has ever been given to the world.

With the influx of the North-men over Europe came a new ideal of the sexual relation, and the wife mounted more into equality with the husband than before. The romance of love, however, still went mainly outside marriage, and may I believe be traced in two chief forms – that of Chivalry, as a chaste and ideal devotion to pure Womanhood ; and that of Minstrelsy, which took quite a different hue, individual and sentimental – the lover and his mistress (she as often as not the wife of another), the serenade, secret amour, & c. – both of which forms of Chivalry and Minstrelsy contain in themselves something new and not quite familiar to antiquity.

Finally in modern times the monogamic union has risen to pre-eminence – the splendid ideal of an equal and life-long attachment between man and wife, fruitful of children in this life, and hopeful of continuance beyond – and has become the great theme of romantic literature, and the climax of a thousand novels and poems. Yet it is just here and to-day, when this ideal after centuries of struggle has established itself, and among the nations that are in the van of civilisation – that we find the doctrine of perfect liberty in the marriage relationship being most successfully preached, and that the communalisation of social life in the future seems likely to weaken the family bond and to relax the obligation of the marriage tie.

If the Greek age, splendid as it was in itself and in its fruits to human progress, did not hold marriage very high, it was partly because the ideal passion of that period, and one which more than all else inspired it, was that of comradeship, or male friendship carried over into the region of love. The two figures of Harmodius and Aristogiton stand at the entrance of Greek history as the type of this passion, bearing its fruit (as Plato throughout maintains is its nature) in united self-devotion to the country's good. The heroic Theban legion, the "sacred band," into which no man might enter without his lover – and which was said to have remained unvanquished till it was annihilated at the battle of Chaeronaea – proves to us how publicly this passion and its place in society were recognised; while its universality and the depth to which it had stirred the Greek mind are indicated by the fact that whole treatises on love, in its spiritual aspect, exist, in which no other form of the sentiment seems to be contemplated; and by the magnificent panorama of Greek statuary, which was obviously to a large extent inspired by it. In fact the most remarkable Society known to history, and its greatest men, can not be properly considered or understood apart from this passion; yet the modern world scarcely recognises it, or if it recognises, does so chiefly to condemn it[2].

Other instances might be quoted to show how differently moral questions are regarded in one age and another – as in the case of Usury, Magic, Suicide, Infanticide, & c. On the whole we pride ourselves (and justly I believe) on the general advance in humanity; yet we know that to-day the merest savages can only shudder at a civilisation whose public opinion allows – as amongst us – the rich to wallow in their wealth while the poor are systematically starving; and it is certain that Vivisection – which on the whole is approved by our educated classes (though not by the healthier sentiment of the uneducated) – would have been stigmatised as one of the most abominable crimes by the ancient Egyptians – if, that is, they could have conceived such a practice possible at all.

But not only do the moral judgments of mankind thus vary from age to age and from race to race, but – what is equally remarkable – they vary to an extraordinary degree from class to class of the same society. If the landlord class regards the poacher as a criminal, the poacher as already hinted looks upon the landlord as a selfish ruffian who has the police on his side; if the respectable shareholder, politely and respectably subsisting on dividends, dismisses navvies and the frequenters of public-houses as disorderly persons; the navvy in return despises the shareholder as a sneaking thief. And it is not easy to see, after all, which is in the right. It is useless to dismiss these discrepancies by supposing that one class in the nation possesses a monopoly of morality and that the other classes simply rail at the virtue they cannot attain to, for this is obviously not the case. It is almost a commonplace, and certainly a fact that cannot be contested, that every class – however sinful or outcast in the eyes of others – contains within its ranks a large proportion of generous, noble, self-sacrificing characters; so that the public opinion of one such class, however different from that of others, cannot at least be invalidated on the above ground. There are plenty of clergymen at this moment who are models of pastors – true shepherds of the people – though a large and increasing section of society persist in regarding priests as a kind of wolves in sheep's clothing. It is not uncommon to meet with professional thieves who are generous and open-handed to the last degree, and ready to part with their last penny to help a comrade in distress; with women living outside the bounds of conventional morality who are strongly religious in sentiment, and who regard atheists as *really* wicked people; with aristocrats who have as stern material in them as quarry-men; and even with bondholders and drawing-room loungers who are as capable of bravery and self-sacrifice as many a pitman or ironworker. Yet all these classes mentioned have their codes of morality, differing in greater or lesser degree from each other; and again the question forces itself upon us: Which of them all is the true and abiding code?

It may be said, with regard to this variation of codes within the same society, that though various codes may exist at the same time, one only is really valid, namely that which has embodied itself in the law – that the others have been rejected because they were unworthy. But when we come to look into this matter of law we see that the plea can hardly be maintained. Law represents from age to age the code of the dominant or ruling class, slowly accumulated, no doubt, and slowly modified, but always added to and always administered by the ruling class. To-day the code of the dominant class may perhaps best be denoted by the word Respectability – and if we ask why this code has to a great extent *overwhelmed* the codes of the other classes and got the law on its side (so far that in the main it characterises those classes who do not conform to it as the criminal classes), the answer can only be: Because it *is* the code of the classes who are in power. Respectability is the code of those who have the wealth and the command, and as these have also the fluent pens and tongues, it is the standard of modern literature and the press. It is not necessarily a better standard than others, but it is the one that happens to be in the ascendant; it is the code of the classes that chiefly represent modern society; it is the code of the Bourgeoisie. It is different from the Feudal code of the past, of the knightly classes, and of Chivalry; it is different from the Democratic code of the future – of brotherhood and of equality; it is the code of the Commercial age and its distinctive watchword is – property.

The Respectability of to-day is the respectability of property. There is nothing so respectable as being well-off. The

Law confirms this: everything is on the side of the rich; justice is too expensive a thing for the poor man. Offences against the person hardly count for so much as those against property. You may beat your wife within an inch of her life and only get three months; but if you steal a rabbit, you may be "sent" for years. So again gambling by thousands on Change is respectable enough, but pitch and toss for halfpence in the streets is low, and must be dealt with by the police; while it is a mere commonplace to say that the high-class swindler is "received" in society from which a more honest but patch-coated brother would infallibly be rejected. As Walt Whitman has it "There is plenty of glamour about the most damnable crimes and hoggish meannesses, special and general, of the feudal and dynastic world over there, with its personnel of lords and queens and courts, so well-dressed and handsome. But the people are ungrammatical, untidy, and their sins gaunt and ill-bred."

Thus we see that though there are for instance in the England of to-day a variety of classes, and a variety of corresponding codes of public opinion and morality, one of these codes, namely that of the ruling class whose watchword is property, is strongly in the ascendant. And we may fairly suppose that in any nation from the time when it first becomes divided into well-marked classes this is or has been the case. In one age – the commercial age – the code of the commercial or money-loving class is dominant; in another – the military – the code of the warrior class is dominant; in another – the religious – the code of the priestly class; and so on. And even before any question of division into classes arises, while races are yet in a rudimentary and tribal state, the utmost diversity of custom and public opinion marks the one from the other.

What, then, are we to conclude from all these variations (and the far greater number which I have not mentioned) of the respect or stigma attaching to the *same* actions, not only among different societies in different ages or parts of the world, but even at anyone time among different classes of the same society? Must we conclude that there is no such thing as a permanent moral code valid for all time; or must we still suppose that there is such a thing – though society has hitherto sought for it in vain?

I think *it* is obvious that there is no such thing as a permanent moral code – at any rate as applying to *actions.* Probably the respect or stigma attaching to particular classes of actions arose from the fact that these classes of actions were – or were thought to be – beneficial or injurious to the society of the time; but it is also clear that this good or bad name once created clings to the action long after the action has ceased in the course of social progress to be beneficial in the one case, or injurious in the other; and indeed long after the thinkers of the race have discovered the discrepancy. And so in a short time arises a great confusion in the popular mind between what is really good or evil for the race and what is reputed to be so – the bolder spirits who try to separate the two having to atone for this confusion by their own martyrdom. It is also pretty clear that the actions which are beneficial or injurious to the race must by the nature of the case vary almost indefinitely with the changing conditions of the life of the race – what is beneficial in one age or under one set of conditions being injurious in another age or under other circumstances – so that a permanent or ever-valid code of moral action is not a thing to be expected, at any rate by those who regard morality as a result of social experience, and as a matter of fact is not a thing that we find existing. And, indeed, of those who regard morals as intuitive, there are few who have thought about the matter who would be inclined to say that any *act* in itself can be either right or wrong. Though there is a superficial judgment of this kind, yet when the matter comes to be looked into the more general consent seems to be that the rightness or wrongness is in the *motive*. To kill (it is said) is not wrong, but to do so with murderous intent is; to take money out of another person's purse is in itself neither moral or immoral – all depends upon whether permission has been given, or on what the relations between the two persons are; and so on. Obviously there is no mere act

65

which under given conditions may not be justified, and equally obviously there is no mere act which under given conditions may not become unjustifiable. To talk, therefore, about virtues and vices as permanent and distinct classes of actions is illusory; there is no such distinction, except so far as a superficial and. transient public opinion creates it. The theatre of morality is in the passions, and there are (it is said) virtuous and vicious passions – eternally distinct from each other.

Here, then, we have abandoned the search for a permanent moral code among the actions; on the understanding that we are more likely to find such a thing among the passions. And I think it would be generally admitted that this is a move in the right direction. There are difficulties however here, and the matter is not one which renders itself up at once. Though, vaguely speaking, some passions seem nobler and more dignified than others, we find it very difficult, in fact impossible, to draw any strict line which shall separate one class, the virtuous, from the other class, the vicious. On the whole we place Prudence, Generosity, Chastity, Reverence, Courage, among the virtues – and their opposites, as Rashness, Miserliness, Incontinence, Arrogance, Timidity, among the vices; yet we do not seem able to say that Prudence is always better than Rashness, Chastity than Incontinence, or Reverence than Arrogance. There are situations in which the less honoured quality is the most in place; and if the extreme of this is undesirable, the extreme of its opposite is undesirable too. Courage, it is commonly said, must not be carried over into foolhardiness; Chastity must not go so far as the monks of the early Church took it, there is a limit to the indulgence of the instinct of Reverence. In fact the less dignified passions are necessary sometimes as a counterbalance and set-off to the more dignified, and a character devoid of them would be very insipid; just as among the members of the body, the less honoured have their place as well as the more honoured, and could not well be discarded[3].

Hence a number of writers, abandoning the attempt to

draw a fixed line between virtuous and vicious passions, have boldly maintained that vices have their place as well as virtues, and that the true salvation lies in the golden mean. The speika and sjoeouuh of the Greeks seem to have pointed to the idea of a blend or harmonious adjustment of all the powers as the perfection of character.

The English word "gentleman" seems to have once conveyed a similar idea. And Emerson, among others, maintains that each vice is only the "excess or acridity of a virtue," and says "the first lesson of history is the good of evil."

According to this view rightness or wrongness cannot be predicated of the passions themselves, but should rather be applied to the use of them, and to the way they are proportioned to each other and to circumstances. As, farther back, we left the region of actions to look for morality in the passions (in the Museum I think) is the following inscription: – "To Aste, for a memorial of her gentleness, Daphnis framed this – having loved her dearly in life, and longing for her now she is dead." that lie behind action, so now we leave the region of the passions to look for it in the power that lies behind the passions and gives them their place. This is a farther move in the same direction as before, and possibly will bring us to a more satisfactory conclusion. There are still difficulties, however – the chief ones lying in the want of definiteness which necessarily attaches to our dealings with these remoter tracts of human nature; and in our own defective knowledge of these tracts.

For these reasons, and as the subject is a complex and difficult one, I would ask the reader to dwell for a few minutes longer on the considerations which show that it is really as impossible to draw a fixed line between moral and immoral passions as it is between moral and immoral actions, and which therefore force us if we are to find any ground of morality at all, to look for it in some further region of our nature.

Plato in his allegory of the soul – in the Phaedrus – though he apparently divides the passions which draw the human chariot into two classes, the heavenward and the earthward – figured by the white horse and the black horse respectively – does not recommend that the black horse should be destroyed or dismissed, but only that he (as well as the white horse) should be kept under due control by the charioteer. By which he seems to intend that there is a power in man which stands above and behind the passions, and under whose control alone the human being can safely move. In fact if the fiercer and so-called more earthly passions were removed, half the driving force would be gone from the chariot of the human soul. Hatred may be devilish at times – but after all the true value of it depends on what you hate, on the use to which the passion is put. Anger, though inhuman at one time is magnificent and divine at another. Obstinacy may be out of place in a drawing-room, but it is the latest virtue on a battle-field when an important position has to be held against the full brunt of the enemy. And Lust, though maniacal and monstrous in its aberrations, cannot in the last resort be separated from its divine companion, Love. To let the more amiable passions have entire sway notoriously does not do: to turn your cheek, too literally, to the smiter, is (*pace* Tolsti) only to encourage smiting; and when society becomes so altruistic that everybody runs to fetch the coal-scuttle we feel sure that something has gone wrong. The white-washed heroes of our biographies with their many virtues and no faults do not please us. We have an impression that the man without faults is, to say the least, a vague, uninteresting being – a picture without light and shade – and the conventional semi-pious classification of character into good and bad qualities (as if the good might be kept and the bad thrown away) seems both inadequate and false.

What the student of human nature rather has to do is not to divide the virtues (so-called) from the vices (so-called), not to separate the black horse and the white horse, but to find out what is the relation of the one to the other – to see the character as a whole, and the mutual interdependence of its different parts – to find out what that power is which constitutes it a unity, whose presence and control makes the man and all his actions "right," and in whose absence (if it is really possible for it to be entirely absent) the man and his actions must be "wrong."

What we call vices, faults, defects, appear often as a kind of limitation: cruelty for instance as a limitation of human sympathy, prejudice as a blindness, a want of discernment; but it is just these limitations – in one form or another – which are the necessary conditions of the appearance of a human being in the world. If we are to act or live at all we must act and live under limits. There must be channels along which the stream is forced to run, else it will spread and lose itself aimlessly in all directions – and turn no mill-wheels. One man is disagreeable and unconciliatory – the directions in which his sympathy goes out to others are few and limited – yet there are situations in life (and everyone must know them) when a man who is *able and willing* to make himself disagreeable is invaluable: when a Carlyle is worth any number of Balaams.

(To be concluded)

Notes

1. Yet there is no doubt that lasting and passionate love may exist between two persons thus nearly related. The danger to the health of the offspring from occasional in-breeding of the kind appears to arise chiefly from the accentuation of infirmities common to the two parents. In a state of society free from the diseases of the civilisation-period, such a danger would be greatly reduced – and this may partly serve to explain the extensive admission of this custom in savagery.

2. Modern writers fixing their regard on the physical side of this love (necessary no doubt here, as elsewhere, to define and corroborate the spiritual) have entered their protest as against the mere obscenity into which the thing fell – for instance in the days of Martial – but have missed the profound significance of the heroic attachment itself. It is, however, with the ideals that we are just now concerned and not with their disintegration.

3. Of course by enlarging indefinitely the definition of any virtue – say Reverence – the word might be got to cover and include all those cases in which its opposite Arrogance (as commonly understood) is desirable. But by that time the word would really have lost its *definition,* and would have ceased to be of any practical use.

Defence of Criminals – Criticism of Immorality II

Sometimes again vices, & c., appear as a kind of raw material from which the other qualities have to be formed and without which, in a sense, they could not exist. Sensuality, for instance, underlies all art and the higher emotions. Timidity is the defect of the sensitive imaginative temperament. Bluntness, stupid candour and want of tact are indispensable in the formation of certain types of Reformers. But what would you have? Would you have a rabbit with the horns of a cow, or a donkey with the disposition of a spaniel? The reformer has not to extirpate his brusqueness and aggressiveness, but to see that he makes good use of these qualities; and the man has not to abolish his sensuality but to redeem it.

And so on. Lecky, in his "History of Morals," shows how in society certain defects necessarily accompany certain excellencies of character. "Had the Irish peasants been less chaste they would have been more prosperous" is his blunt assertion -which he supports by the contention that their early marriages (which render the said virtue possible) "are the most conspicuous proofs of the national improvidence, and one of the most fatal obstacles to industrial prosperity." Similarly, he says that the gambling table fosters a moral nerve and calmness "scarcely exhibited in equal perfection in any other sphere" – a fact which Bret Harte has finely illustrated in his character of Mr. John Oakhurst in the "Outcasts of Poker Flat;" also that "the promotion of industrial veracity is probably the single form in which the growth of manufactures exercises a favourable influence upon morals;" while on the other hand, "Trust in Providence, content and resignation in extreme poverty and suffering, the most genuine amiability and the most sincere readiness to assist their brethren, an adherence to their religious opinions which no persecutions and no bribes can shake, a capacity for heroic, transcendent and prolonged self-sacrifice, may be found in some nations, in men who are habitual liars and habitual cheats." Again he points out that thriftiness and forethought – which, in an industrial civilisation like ours, are looked upon as duties "of the very highest order" – have at other times (when the teaching was "take no thought for the morrow," been regarded as quite the reverse, and concludes with the general remark that as society advances there is some loss for every gain that is made, and with the special indictment against "civilisation" that it is not favourable to the production of "self-sacrifice, enthusiasm, reverence or chastity."

The point of all which is that the so-called vices and defects – whether we regard them as limitations or whether we regard them as raw materials of character, whether we regard them in the individual solely or whether we regard them in their relation to society – are necessary elements of human life, elements without which the so-called virtues could not exist; and that therefore it is quite impossible to separate vices and virtues into distinct classes with the latent idea involved that one class may be retained and the other in course of time got rid of. Defects and bad qualities will not be treated so – they clamour for their rights and will not be denied; they effect a lodgement in us, and we have to put up with them. Like the grain of sand in the oyster, we are forced to make pearls of them.

These are the precipices and chasms which give form to the mountain. Who wants a mountain sprawling indifferently out on all sides, without angle or break, like the oceanic tide-wave of which one cannot say whether it is a hill or a plain? And if you want to grow a lily, chastely white and filling the air with its fragrance, will you not bury the bulb of it deep in the dirt to begin with?

Acknowledging then that it is impossible to hold permanently to any distinction between good and bad passions, there remains nothing for it but to accept both, and to *make use*

72

of them – redeeming them, both good and bad, from their narrowness and limitation by so doing-to make use of them in the service of humanity. For as dirt is only matter in the wrong place, so evil in man consists only in actions or passions which are uncontrolled by the human within him, and undedicated to its service. The evil consists not in the actions or passions themselves, but in the fact that they are inhumanly used. The most unblemished virtue erected into a barrier between oneself and a suffering brother or sister – the whitest marble image, howsoever lovely, set up in the Holy Place of the temple of Man, where the spirit alone should dwell – becomes blasphemy and a pollution.

Wherein exactly this human service consists is another question. It may be, and as the reader would gather, probably is, a matter which at the last eludes definition. But though it may elude exact statement, that is no reason why approximations should not be made to the statement of it; nor is its ultimate elusiveness of intellectual definition any proof that it may not become a real and vital force within the man, and underlying inspiration of his actions. To take the two considerations in order; in the first place, as we saw from the beginning, the experience of society is continually leading it to classify actions into beneficial and harmful, good and bad; and thus moral codes are formed which eat their way from the outside into the individual man and become part of him. These codes may be looked upon as approximations in each age to a statement of human service: but, as we have seen, they are by the nature of the case very imperfect; and since the very conditions of the problem are continually changing, it seems obvious that a final and absolute solution of it by this method is impossible. The second way in which man works towards a solution is by the expansion and growth of his own consciousness, and is ultimately by far the most important – though the two methods have doubtless continually to be corrected by each other. In fact as man actually forms a part of society externally, so he comes to know and *feel* himself a part of society through his inner nature. Gradually, and in the lapse of ages, through the development of his sympathetic relation with his fellows, the individual man enters into a wider and wider circle of life – the joys and sorrows, the experiences, of his fellows become his own joys and sorrows, his own experiences – he passes into a life which is larger than his own individual life – forces flow in upon him which determine his actions, not for results which return to him directly, but for results which can only return to him indirectly and through others; at last the ground of humanity as it were reveals itself within him, the region of human equality – and his actions come to flow directly from the very same source which regulates and inspires the whole movement of society. At this point the problem is solved. The growth has taken place from within; it is not of the nature of an external compulsion, but of an inward compunction. By actual consciousness the man has taken on an ever-enlarging life, and at last the life of humanity, which has no fixed form, no ever-valid code; but is itself the true life, surpassing definition, yet inspiring all actions and passions, all codes and forms, and determining at last their place.

It is the gradual growth at this supreme life in each individual which is the great and indeed the only hope of Society – it is that for which Society exists: a life which so far from dwarfing individuality enhances immensely its power, causing the individual to move with the weight of the universal behind him – and exalting what were once his little peculiarities and defects into the splendid manifestations of his humanity.

To return then for a moment to the practical bearing at this on the question before us, we see that so soon as we have abandoned all codes of morals there remains nothing for us but to put *all* our qualities and defects to human use, and to redeem them by so doing. Our defects are our entrances into life, and the gateway of all our dealings with others. Think what it is to be plain and *homely*. The very word suggests an endearment, and a liberty of access denied to the faultlessly handsome. Our very evil passions, so-called, are not things to be ashamed of, but things to look straight in the face and to see what they are good for – for a use can be found for them, that is certain. The man should see that he is worthy of his passion, as the mountain should rear its crest conformable to the height of the precipice which bounds it. Is it women? let him see that he is a magnanimous lover. Is it ambition? let him take care that it be a grand one. Is it laziness? let it redeem him from the folly of unrest, to become heaven-reflecting like a lake among the hills. It is closefistedness? let it become the nurse of a true economy.

The more complicated, pronounced or awkward the defect is the finer will be the result when it has been thoroughly worked up. Love of approbation is difficult to deal with. Through Sloughs of duplicity, of concealment, of vanity, it leads its victim. It sucks his sturdy self-life, and leaves him flattened and bloodless. Yet once mastered, once fairly torn out, cudgelled, and left bleeding on the road (for this probably has to be done with every vice or virtue some time or other) – it will rise up and follow you, carrying a magic key round its neck – meek and serviceable now instead of dangerous and demoniac as before.

Deceit is difficult to deal with. In some sense it is the worst fault that can be. It seems to disorganise and ultimately to destroy the character. Yet I am bold to say that this defect has its uses. Severely examined perhaps it will be found that no one can live a day free from it. And beyond that – is not "a noble dissimulation" part and parcel of the very greatest characters: like Socrates, "the white soul in satyr form"? When the divine has descended among men has it not always like Moses worn a veil before its face? and what is Nature herself but one long and organised system of deception?

Veracity has an opposite effect. It knits all the elements of a man's character – rendering him solid rather than fluid; yet carried out too literally and pragmatically it condenses and solidifies the character overmuch, making the man woodeny and angular. And even of that essential Truth (truth to the inward and ideal perfection) which more than anything else perhaps *constitutes,* a man – it is to be remembered that even here there must be a limitation. No man can in act or externally be quite true to the ideal – though in spirit he may be. If he is to live in this world and be mortal, it must be by virtue of some partiality, some defect.

And so again – since there is an analogy between the individual and society – may we not conclude that as the individual has ultimately to recognise his so-called evil passions and find a place and a use for them, society also has to recognise its so-called criminals and discern their place and use? The artist does not omit shadows from his canvas; and the wise statesman will not try to abolish the criminal from society – less haply he be found to have abolished the driving force from his social machine.[1]

From what has now been said it is quite clear that the criminal is not a criminal because he violates any eternal code of morality – for there exists no such thing – but because he violates the ruling code of his time, and this depends largely on the ideal of the time. The Spartans appear to have permitted theft because they thought that thieving habits in the community fostered military dexterity and discouraged the accumulation of private wealth. They looked upon the latter as a great evil. But to-day the accumulation of private wealth is our great good and the thief is looked upon as the evil. When, however, we find, as the historians of to-day teach us, that society is now probably passing through a parenthetical stage of private property from a stage of communism in the past to a stage of more highly developed communism in the future, it becomes clear that the thief (and the poacher before-mentioned) is that person who is protesting against the too exclusive domination of a passing ideal. What ever should we do without him? He is keeping open for us, as Hinton I think expresses it, the path to a regenerate society, and is more useful to that end than many a platform orator. He it is that makes Care to sit upon the crupper of Wealth, and so, in course of time, causes the burden and bother

76

of private property to become so intolerable that society gladly casts it down on common ground. Vast as is the machinery of Law, and multifarious the ways in which it seeks to crush the thief, it has signally failed, and fails ever more and more. The thief will win. He will get what he wants, but (as usual in human life!) in a way and in a form very different from what he expected.

And when we regard the thief in himself, we cannot say that we find him less human than other classes of society. The sentiment of large bodies of thieves is highly communistic among themselves; and if they thus represent a survival from an earlier age, they might also be looked upon as the precursors of a better age in the future. They have their pals in every town, with runs and refuges always open, and are lavish and generous to a degree to their own kind. And if they look upon the rich as their natural enemies and fair prey, a view which it might be difficult to gainsay, many of them at any rate are animated by a good deal of the Robin Hood spirit, and are really helpful to the poor.

I need not I think quote that famous passage from Lecky in which he shows how the prostitute, through centuries of suffering and ill-fame, has borne the curse and contempt of society in order that her more fortunate sister might rejoice in the achievement of a pure marriage. The ideal of a monogamic union has been established in a sense directly by the slur cast upon the free woman. If, however, as many people think, a certain latitude in sexual relations is not only admissible but in the long run, and within bounds, desirable, it becomes clear that the prostitute is that person who against heavy odds, and at the cost of a real degradation to herself, has clung to a tradition which, in itself good, might otherwise have perished in the face of our devotion to the splendid ideal of the exclusive marriage. There has been a time in history when the prostitute (if the word can properly be used in this connection) has been glorified, consecrated to the temple-service and honoured of men and gods (the hierodouloi of the Greeks, the kodeshoth and kodeshim of the Bible, & c.) There has also been a time when she has been scouted and reviled. In the future there will come a time when, as free companion, really free from the curse of modern commercialism, and sacred and respected once more, she will again be accepted by society and take her place with the rest.

And so with other cases. On looking back into history we find that almost every human impulse has at some age been held in esteem and allowed full play; thus man came to recognise its beauty and value. But then lest it should come (as it surely would) to tyrannise over the rest, it has been dethroned, and so in a later age the same quality is scouted and banned. Last of all it has to find its perfect human use and to take its place with the rest. Up to the age of civilisation (according to Lewis Morgan[2]) the early tribes of mankind, though limited each in their habits, were essentially democratical in structure. In fact nothing had occurred to make them otherwise. Each member stood on a footing of equality with the rest; no man had in his hands an arbitrary power over others; and the tribal life and standard ruled supreme. And when, in the future and on a much higher plane, the true Democracy comes, this equality which has so long been in abeyance will be restored, not only among men but also, in a sense, among all the passions and qualities of manhood, none will be allowed to tyrannise over others, but all will have to be subject to the supreme life of humanity. The chariot of Man, instead of two horses will have a thousand; but they will all be under control of the charioteer. Meanwhile it may not be extravagant to suppose that all through the civilisation-period the so-called criminals are keeping open the possibility of a return to this state of society. They are preserving, in a rough and unattractive husk it may be, the precious seed of a life which is to come in the future; and are as necessary and integral a part of society in the long run as the most respected and most honoured of its members at present.

The upshot, then, of it all is that "morals" as a code of action have to be discarded. There exists no such code, at any rate for permanent use. One age, one race, one class, one family, may have a code which the users of it consider valid, but only they consider it valid, and they only for a time. The Decalogue may have been a rough and useful ready-reckoner for the Israelites; but to us it admits of so many exceptions and interpretations that it is practically worthless. "Thou shalt not steal." Exactly; but who is to decide, as we saw at the outset, in what "stealing" consists? The question is too complicated to admit of an answer. And when we *have* caught our half-starved tramp taking a loaf, and are ready to condemn him, lo! Lycurgus pats him on the back, and the modern philosopher tells him that he is keeping open the path to a regenerate society! If the tramp had also been a philosopher he would, perhaps, have done the same act not merely for his own benefit but for that of society, he would have committed a crime in order to save mankind.

There is nothing left but Humanity. Since there is no ever-valid code of morals we must sadly confess that there is no means of proving ourselves right and our neighbours wrong. In fact the very act of thinking whether *we* are right (which implies a sundering of ourselves, even in thought, from others) itself introduces the element of wrongness; and if we are ever to *be* "right," at all, it must be at some moment when we fail to notice it – when we have forgotten our apartness from others and have entered into the great region of human equality. Equality – in that region all human defects are redeemed; they all find their place. To love your neighbour *as* yourself is the whole law and the prophets; to feel that you are "equal" with others, that their lives are as your life, that your life is as theirs – even in what trifling degree we may experience such things – is to enter into another life which includes both sides; it is to pass beyond the sphere of moral distinctions, and to trouble oneself no more with them. Between lovers there are no duties and no rights; and in the life of humanity, there is only an instinctive mutual service expressing itself in whatever way may be best at the time. Nothing is forbidden, there is nothing which may not serve. The law of Equality is perfectly flexible, is adaptable to all times and places, finds a place for all the elements of character, justifies and redeems them all without exception; and to live by it is perfect freedom. Yet not a law; but rather, as said, a new life, transcending the individual life, working through it from within, lifting the self into another sphere, beyond corruption, far over the world of sorrow.

The effort to make a distinction between acting for self and acting for one's neighbour is the basis of "morals." As long as a man feels an ultimate antagonism between himself and society, as long as he tries to hold his own life as a thing apart from that of others, so long must the question arise whether he will act for self or for those others. Hence flow a long array of terms – distinctions of right and wrong, duty, selfishness, self-renunciation, altruism, etc. But when he discovers that there is no ultimate antagonism between himself and society; when he finds that the gratification of every desire which he has or can have may be rendered social, or beneficial to his fellows, by being used at the right time and place, and on the other hand that every demand made upon him by society will and must gratify some portion of his nature, some desire of his heart – why, all the distinctions collapse again; they do not hold water any more. A larger life descends upon him, which includes both sides, and prompts actions in accordance with an unwritten and unimagined law. Such actions will sometimes be accounted "selfish" by the world; sometimes they will be accounted "unselfish"; but they are neither, or – if you like – both; and he who does them concerns himself not with the names that may be given to them. The law of Equality includes all the moral codes, and is the stand-point which they cannot reach, but which they all aim at.

Of course this reconcilement of the individual with society – of the unit man with the mass-Man – involves the subordination of the desires, their subjection to the true Man. And this is a most important point. It is no easy lapse that is here suggested, from morality into a mere jungle of human passion; but a toilsome and long ascent, involving for a time at any rate the severest self-control into ascendancy over the passions; it involves the complete mastery, one by one, of them all; and the recognition and allowance of them only because they are mastered. And it is just this training and subjection of the passions – as of winged horses which are to draw the human chariot – which necessarily forms such a long and painful process of human evolution. The old moral codes are a part of this process; but they go on the plan of extinguishing some of the passions – seeing that it is sometimes easier to shoot a restive horse than to ride him. We however do not want to be lords of dead carrion but of living powers; and every steed that we can add to our chariot makes our progress through creation so much the more splendid, providing Phoebus indeed hold the reins, and not the incapable Phaeton.

And by becoming thus one with the social self, the individual instead of being crushed is made far vaster, far grander than before. The renunciation (if it must be so called) which he has to accept in abandoning merely individual ends is immediately compensated by the far more vivid life he now enters into. For every force of his nature can now be utilised. Planting himself out by contrast he stands all the firmer because he has a left foot as well as a right, and when he acts, he acts not halfheartedly as one afraid, but as it were with the whole weight of humanity behind him. In abandoning his exclusive individuality he becomes for the first time a real and living individual; and in accepting as his own the life of others he becomes aware of a life in himself that has no limit and no end. That the self of anyone man is capable of an infinite gradation from the most petty and exclusive existence to the most magnificent and inclusive seems almost a truism. The one extreme is disease and death, the other is life everlasting. When the tongue for example – which is a member of the body – regards itself as a purely separate existence for itself alone, it makes a mistake, it suffers an illusion, and descends into its pettiest life. What is the consequence? Thinking that it exists apart from the other members, it selects food just such as shall

81

gratify its most local self; it endeavors just to titillate its own sense of taste: and living and acting thus, ere long it ruins that very sense of taste, poisons the system with improper food, and brings about disease and death. Yet if healthy how does the tongue act? Why, it does not run counter to its own sense of taste, or stultify itself. It does not talk about sacrificing its own inclinations for the good of the body and the other members; but it just acts as being one in interest with them and they with it. For the tongue *is* a muscle, and therefore what feeds it feeds all the other muscles; and the membrane of the tongue *is* a prolongation of the membrane of the stomach, and that is how the tongue knows what the stomach will like; and the tongue is nerves and blood, and so the tongue may act for nerves and blood all over the body, and so on. Therefore the tongue may enter into a wider life than that represented by the mere local sense of taste, and experiences more pleasure often in the drinking of a glass of water which the whole body wants, than in the daintiest Sweetmeat which is for itself alone.

Exactly so man in a healthy state does not act for himself alone, practically cannot do so. Nor does he talk cant about "serving his neighbours" & c. But he simply acts for them as well as for himself, because they are part and parcel of his life – bone of his bone and flesh of his flesh; and in doing so he enters into a wider life, finds a more perfect pleasure, and becomes more really a man than ever before. Every man contains in himself the elements of all the rest of humanity. They lie in the background; but they are there. In the front he has his own special faculty developed – his individual facade, with its projects, plans and purposes: but behind sleeps the demos-life with far vaster projects and purposes. Some time or other to every man must come the consciousness of this vaster life.

The true Democracy, wherein this larger life will rule society from within – obviating the need of an external government – and in which all characters and qualities will be recognised and have their freedom, waits (a hidden but necessary result of evolution) in the constitution of human nature itself. In the pre-civilisation period these vexed questions of "morals" practically did not exist; simply because in that period the individual was one with his tribe and moved (unconsciously) by the larger life of his tribe. And in the post-civilisation period, when the true Democracy comes again, they will not exist, because then the man will know himself a part of humanity at large, and will be consciously moved by forces belonging to these vaster regions of his being. The moral codes and questionings belong to Civilisation, they are part of the struggle, the suffering, and the alienation from true life, which that term implies.

EDWARD CARPENTER.

Notes

1. The derivation of the word "wicked" seems uncertain. May it be suggested that it is connected with "wick" or "quick" meaning *alive*?

2. See "Ancient Society," *passim*.

The Value of Value Theory

One word more on this ever interesting subject. That Karl Marx had, metaphorically speaking, his tongue in his cheek when he propounded his statement of the theory of value is, I should say, more than probable. It seems hardly possible that its defects (for I take it they are more than one) were not patent to his shrewd untiring mind; but for his purpose – namely, the substitution of a society founded on a basis of labour for the old order or disorder of mere *laissez-faire* – it seemed obviously *necessary* to make labour the measure of value. Probably (*pace* Shaw and the rest) it is the most important element in value – though, of course, there are other elements. Marx however made it the sole determinant of value. But whose labour? What labour? Clearly not the labour of this or that individual. A brief but carefully steered analysis answered this question, and Marx returned with an abstraction "socially necessary labour," and offered this as the test and measure of value. The Socialist party naturally accepted, without question, from their Aristotle a *dictum* so exactly suited to their wants, nor stopped to enquire too closely whether it had any meaning or not.

That was all right enough. We can understand the position of Marx. He had to provide a theory for a particular purpose, and he provided it. But what is the position of Hyndman? Here we are puzzled. There are two alternatives. Either – as Shaw appears to believe – he really thinks Marx had no reserve in his own mind about the theory, and his, Hyndman's, attempted re-statement of it in the April No. of To-DAY is perfectly frank and guile-less; or else – and I incline to this view – he deems the pious fraud of Marx still necessary, and believes that even at this late hour an enlightened public may by mock thunders and *ex-Cathedra* threats be made to accept it. Neither supposition is, I fear, altogether creditable to the Hyndmanic intelligence, though the latter is perhaps the

85

most creditable – and that is why I am disposed to adopt it.

Now to come to our friend Shaw. Sadly near the conclusion of his entertaining article, he unfolds in a few words his (plus Wicksteed and Jevons) theory of value. He says – what is perfectly true – that Marx, in generalising the specific labour involved in making such commodities as boots and tables into a common element, "abstract human labour," which he regarded as the measure of value of these commodities, neglected the fact that the same process might be applied to the specific *utilities* of boots and tables – which might thus be generalised into a common "abstract desirability." And he then and there maintains; that "this abstract desirability is the true basis, ground, substance, final cause, efficient cause – what you please – of value."

And it is here that I am reluctantly compelled to conclude that Shaw, like Marx and Hyndman before him, is playing a little game with us. Apart from the suspicious appearance of such words as "substance," "final cause," and "what you please," in a scientific treatise by a Fabian philosopher – there remains the obvious and indelible fact that the phrase "abstract desirability" itself has absolutely no meaning. It has no meaning which can in any way be defined, measured, or made clearly intelligible. It has no more meaning than Marx's "abstract human labour" or "socially necessary labour" and those phrases are incapable of any clear definition. The only attempt, as far as I know, at an exact definition of them that Marx makes is in the following passage of "Capital" (I have only the French edition) "Le temps socialement nécessaire à la production des marchandises est celui qu'exige tout travail, exécuté avec le degré moyen d'habileté et d'intensité et dans les conditions qui, par rapport au milieu social donné, sont normales." The more you think about such a sentence the more clearly you see that it raises greater difficulties than it disposes of; and if Hyndman's efforts to attach an exact meaning to it and the other phrases are the efforts of an intelligent human being, those efforts only show that no such meaning *can* be attached to them. The same with Shaw's "abstract desirability"; only he wisely, in the present article, does not attempt to indicate what he means by the phrase. The only remark he ventures is this:- "And whilst it (*i.e.* the abstract desirability) remains constant, no alteration of the labour-time socially necessary to produce the commodity can alter its exchange-value one jot." Now what does that mean? *Whilst the abstract desirability remains constant.* Just think for a moment. What is the abstract desirability of your boot for instance? and what is meant by the abstract desirability of a boot or boots remaining constant? Say, Shaw, what *do* you mean?

Abstract desirability, mark you! Desirability to myself I can understand. Every hour I compare the desirability of objects to myself. I *choose* (a concrete act). But abstract desirability, as among millions of people? Here we come to a full stop. So of labour-cost. Any individual can say whether of two objects costs *him* most labour to make, but which contains most abstract human labour, and in what proportions. . ? All this is only a return, under modern guise, to the quiddities of the Schoolmen. That this object is desired by, and has a specific value to me, because of the abstract desirability residing in it, is just the same as saying that water drowns me because of its aquosity. It is either stating an individual and measurable concrete fact over again in a vaguer and more general, but less measurable, form, or it is nonsense. There is no means of measuring these abstractions except by the concrete cases they profess to explain. "Why do these two commodities exchange for each other?" answer, "Because of a certain relation between – their abstract deslrabilities." "How do you know that this relation exists between their abstract desirabilities?" "Because they exchange for each other." There is no other way. Naturally Shaw does not put his argument in this form, but it is implied in the statements he does make. Of course if there were any *a priori* method of measuring the abstract desirabilities of Shaw or the final utilities[1] of Jevons these remarks would not apply

– but is there? The Jevonian theory, though more logical in *form* than the Marxian, is less satisfactory in *content,* It is conceivable, as Hyndman suggests, that in some future state of Society the labour-cost of a commodity *may* be calculable independently of its actual exchange value, and so become a real basis for its exchange with other commodities (only this would not probably be of much use, as by that time exchange generally would have ceased to exist); but it is hardly conceivable that the final utilities of commodities can ever be calculated beforehand. Notwithstanding hopes to the contrary somewhat faintly expressed by Jevons himself, his phi's and psi's will I fear remain psi's and phi's to all eternity. On p.148 – a few pages after the article in To-Day to which we are referring – we are told by a writer, apparently representing the Fabian society, that a phrase like "in the abstract is wholly unmeaning and belongs to the pre-Fabian era." Surely this writer does not look upon our friend Shaw as a sort of economic pterodactyle.

And now to come to Carpenter – I confess the conclusion is unsatisfactory. It is this. There is *no* theory in these matters which will permanently hold water. (For every theory has to be got at through methods of generalisation similar to the above, by which concrete particulars are abstracted into large but unmeaning concepts – and therefore condemns itself to leakage beforehand – as will be seen perhaps in post-Fabian ages.) In any concrete case of exchange the individuals concerned can and do measure and compare the desirabilities (to them) and the labour-costs (to them), and other attributes besides, of the articles concerned, and do so contribute towards the determination of the relative values of the articles. And, doubtless, all these individual forces over large areas of society do have general resultants which though constantly fluctuating may be said at any one time to *tend* towards fixed determinations or values. More than that we cannot say for certain. We naturally form theories as to what forces are most important in producing such determinations, but the problem obviously involves endless elements of human nature and is remote from solution. A theory is necessary to think by. We must have generalisations for daily use; sometimes it is convenient to generalise the facts of exchange on a basis of labour, sometimes on a basis of utility (final or other), sometimes on a basis of custom, and so on. These different aspects of the problem vary in relative importance at different times and places, and according to the facts envisaged; and one theory may involve fewer untenable positions than another, but it is certain that none is, or can be, impregnable.

The moral of it all is that a doctrine of economics – like a Queen Bess musket – is a very useful thing provided you can make your opponent believe it is dangerous. If Hyndman and Shaw, with their "scientific Socialisms" and other blunderbusses, have succeeded in frightening the bourgeois multitude in the direction in which we wish it to go – what is that but matter of rejoicing to us. Probably none know better than the bearers of these weapons that they are weak in the breach; but if they *look* deadly that is all that is required. Let us congratulate our friends that they have done such valiant service in the cause without having, on the whole, been seriously injured by their own firearms.

EDWARD CARPENTER

Notes

1. Jevons, in fixing our attention on the final moment in the act of exchange, did I take it do a vast service, but this was really independent of his use of the term *utility.*

The Intermediate Sex

"Urning men and women, on whose book of life Nature has written her new word which sounds so strange to us, bear such storm and stress within them, such ferment and fluctuation, so much complex material having its outlet only towards the future; their individualities are so rich and many-sided, and withal so little understood, that it is impossible to characterise them adequately in a few sentences."–Otto de Joux. In late years (and since the arrival of the New Woman amongst us) many things in the relation of men and women to each other have altered, or at any rate become clearer. The growing sense of equality in habits and customs–university studies, art, music, politics, the bicycle, etc.–all these things have brought about a rapprochement between the sexes. If the modern woman is a little more masculine in some ways than her predecessor, the modern man (it is to be hoped), while by no means effeminate, is a little more sensitive in temperament and artistic in feeling than the original John Bull. It is beginning to be recognised that the sexes do not or should not normally form two groups hopelessly isolated in habit and feeling from each other, but that they rather represent the two poles of one group–which is the human race; so that while certainly the extreme specimens at either pole are vastly divergent, there are great numbers in the middle region who (though differing corporeally as men and women) are by emotion and temperament very near to each other. We all know women with a strong dash of the masculine temperament, and we all know men whose almost feminine sensibility and intuition seem to belie their bodily form. Nature, it might appear, in mixing the elements which go to compose each individual, does not always keep her two groups of ingredients–which represent the two sexes– properly apart, but often throws them crosswise in a somewhat baffling manner, now this way and now that; yet wisely, we must think–for if a severe distinction of elements were always maintained the two sexes would soon drift into far latitudes and absolutely cease to understand each other. As it is, there are some remarkable and (we think) indispensable types of character in whom there is such a union or balance of the feminine and masculine qualities that these people become to a great extent the interpreters of men and women to each other.

There is another point which has become clearer of late. For as people are beginning to see that the sexes form in a certain sense a continuous group, so they are beginning to see that Love and Friendship–which have been so often set apart from each other as things distinct–are in reality closely related and shade imperceptibly into each other. Women are beginning to demand that Marriage shall mean Friendship as well as Passion; that a comrade-like Equality shall be included in the word Love; and it is recognised that from the one extreme of a "Platonic" friendship (generally between persons of the same sex) up to the other extreme of passionate love (generally between persons of opposite sex) no hard and fast line can at any point be drawn effectively separating the different kinds of attachment. We know, in fact, of Friendships so romantic in sentiment that they verge into love; we know of Loves so intellectual and spiritual that they hardly dwell in the sphere of Passion.

A moment's thought will show that the general conceptions indicated above–if anywhere near the truth –point to an immense diversity of human temperament and character in matters relating to sex and love; but though such diversity has probably always existed, it has only in comparatively recent times become a subject of study.

More than thirty years ago, however, an Austrian writer, K. H. Ulrichs, drew attention in a series of pamphlets (Memnon, Ara Spei, Inclusa, etc.) to the existence of a class of people who strongly illustrate the above remarks, and with whom specially this paper is concerned. He pointed out that there were people born in such a position—as it were on the dividing line between the sexes—that while belonging distinctly to one sex as far as their bodies are concerned they may be said to belong mentally and emotionally to the other; that there were men, for instance, who might be described as of feminine soul enclosed in a male body (anima muliebris in corpore virili inclusa), or in other cases, women whose definition would be just the reverse. And he maintained that this doubleness of nature was to a great extent proved by the special direction of their love- sentiment. For in such cases, as indeed might be expected, the (apparently) masculine person instead of forming a love-union with a female tended to contract romantic friendships with one of his own sex; while the apparently feminine would, instead of marrying in the usual way, devote herself to the love of another feminine.

People of this kind (i.e., having this special variation of the love-sentiment) he called Urnings; and though we are not obliged to accept his theory about the crosswise connexion between "soul" and "body," since at best these words are somewhat vague and indefinite; yet his work was important because it was one of the first attempts, in modern times, to recognise the existence of what might be called an Intermediate sex, and to give at any rate some explanation of it.

Since that time the subject has been widely studied and written about by scientific men and others, especially on the Continent (though in England it is still comparatively unknown), and by means of an extended observation of present-day cases, as well as the indirect testimony of the history and literature of past times, quite a body of general conclusions has been arrived at—of which I propose in the following pages to give some slight account.

Contrary to the general impression, one of the first points that emerges from this study is that "Urnings," or Uranians, are by no means so very rare; but that they form, beneath the surface of society, a large class. It remains difficult, however, to get an exact statement of their numbers; and this for more than one reason: partly because, owing to the want of any general understanding of their case, these folk tend to conceal their true feelings from all but their own kind, and indeed often deliberately act in such a manner as to lead the world astray– (whence it arises that a normal man living in a certain society will often refuse to believe that there is a single Urning in the circle of his acquaintance, while one of the latter, or one that understands the nature, living in the same society, can count perhaps a score or more)–and partly because it is indubitable that the numbers do vary very greatly, not only in different countries but even in different classes in the same country. The consequence of all this being that we have estimates differing very widely from each other. Dr. Grabowsky, a well-known writer in Germany, quotes figures (which we think must be exaggerated) as high as one man in every 22, while Dr. Albert Moll (Die Conträre Sexualempfindung, chap. 3) gives estimates varying from 1 in every 50 to as low as 1 in every 500. These figures apply to such as are exclusively of the said nature, i.e., to those whose deepest feelings of love and friendship go out only to persons of their own sex. Of course, if in addition are included those double-natured people (of whom there is a great number) who experience the normal attachment, with the homogenic tendency in less or greater degree superadded, the estimates must be greatly higher.

In the second place it emerges (also contrary to the general impression) that men and women of the exclusively Uranian type are by no means necessarily morbid in any way– unless, indeed, their peculiar temperament be pronounced in itself morbid. Formerly it was assumed, as a matter of course, that the type was merely a result of disease and degeneration; but now with the examination of the actual facts it appears that, on the contrary, many are fine, healthy specimens of their sex, muscular and well-developed in body, of powerful brain, high standard of conduct, and with nothing abnormal or morbid of any kind observable in their physical structure or constitution. This is of course not true of all, and there still remain a certain number of cases of weakly type to support the neuropathic view. Yet it is very noticeable that this view is much less insisted on by the later writers than by the earlier. It is also worth noticing that it is now acknowledged that even in the most healthy cases the special affectional temperament of the "Intermediate" is, as a rule, ineradicable; so much so that when (as in not a few instances) such men and women, from social or other considerations, have forced themselves to marry and even have children, they have still not been able to overcome their own bias, or the leaning after all of their life-attachment to some friend of their own sex.

This subject, though obviously one of considerable interest and importance, has been hitherto, as I have pointed out, but little discussed in this country, partly owing to a certain amount of doubt and distrust which has, not unnaturally perhaps, surrounded it. And certainly if the men and women born with the tendency in question were only exceedingly rare, though it would not be fair on that account to ignore them, yet it would hardly be necessary to dwell at great length on their case. But as the class is really, on any computation, numerous, it becomes a duty for society not only to understand them but to help them to understand themselves.

For there is no doubt that in many cases people of this kind suffer a great deal from their own temperament–and yet, after all, it is possible that they may have an important part to play in the evolution of the race. Anyone who realises what Love is, the dedication of the heart, so profound, so absorbing, so mysterious, so imperative, and always just in the noblest natures so strong, cannot fail to see how difficult, how tragic even, must often be the fate of those whose deepest feelings are destined from the earliest days to be a riddle and a stumbling-block, unexplained to themselves, passed over in silence by others. To call people of such temperament "morbid," and so forth, is of no use. Such a term is, in fact, absurdly inapplicable to many, who are among the most active, the most amiable and accepted members of society; besides, it forms no solution of the problem in question, and only amounts to marking down for disparagement a fellow-creature who has already considerable difficulties to contend with. Says Dr. Moll, "Anyone who has seen many Urnings will probably admit that they form a by no means enervated human group; on the contrary, one finds powerful, healthy-looking folk among them;" but in the very next sentence he says that they "suffer severely" from the way they are regarded; and in the manifesto of a considerable community of such people in Germany occur these words, "The rays of sunshine in the night of our existence are so rare, that we are responsive and deeply grateful for the least movement, for every single voice that speaks in our favour in the forum of mankind."

In dealing with this class of folk, then, while I do not deny that they present a difficult problem, I think that just for that very reason their case needs discussion. It would be a great mistake to suppose that their attachments are necessarily sexual, or connected with sexual acts. On the contrary (as abundant evidence shows), they are often purely emotional in their character; and to confuse Uranians (as is so often done) with libertines having no law but curiosity in self- indulgence is to do them a great wrong. At the same time, it is evident that their special temperament may sometimes cause them difficulty in regard to their sexual relations. Into this subject we need not just now enter. But we may point out how hard it is, especially for the young among them, that a veil of complete silence should be drawn over the subject, leading to the most painful misunderstandings, and perversions and confusions of mind; and that there should be no hint of guidance; nor any recognition of the solitary and really serious inner struggles they may have to face! If the problem is a difficult one–as it undoubtedly is–the fate of those people is already hard who have to meet it in their own persons, without their suffering in addition from the refusal of society to give them any help, It is partly for these reasons, and to throw a little light where it may be needed, that I have thought it might be advisable in this paper simply to give a few general characteristics of the Intermediate types.

As indicated then already, in bodily structure there is, as a rule, nothing to distinguish the subjects of our discussion from ordinary men and women; but if we take the general mental characteristics it appears from almost universal testimony that the male tends to be of a rather gentle, emotional disposition– with defects, if such exist, in the direction of subtlety, evasiveness, timidity, vanity, etc.; while the female is just the opposite, fiery, active, bold and truthful, with defects running to brusqueness and coarseness. Moreover, the mind of the former is generally intuitive and instinctive in its perceptions, with more or less of artistic feeling; while the mind of the latter is more logical, scientific, and precise than usual with the normal woman. So marked indeed are these general characteristics that sometimes by means of them (though not an infallible guide) the nature of the boy or girl can be detected in childhood, before full development has taken place; and needless to say it may often be very important to be able to do this.

It was no doubt in consequence of the observation of these signs that K. H. Ulrichs proposed his theory; and though the theory, as we have said, does not by any means meet all the facts, still it is perhaps not without merit, and may be worth bearing in mind.

In the case, for instance, of a woman of this temperament (defined we suppose as "a male soul in a female body") the theory helps us to understand how it might be possible for her to fall bona fide in love with another woman. Krafft-Ebing gives the case of a lady (A.), 28 years of age, who fell deeply in love with a younger one (B.). "I loved her divinely," she said. They lived together, and the union lasted four years, but was then broken by the marriage of B. A. suffered in consequence from frightful depression; but in the end–though without real love–got married herself. Her depression however only increased and deepened into illness.

The doctors, when consulted, said that all would be well if she could only have a child. The husband, who loved his wife sincerely, could not understand her enigmatic behaviour. She was friendly to him, suffered his caresses, but for days afterwards remained "dull, exhausted, plagued with irritation of the spine, and nervous." Presently a journey of the married pair led to another meeting with the female friend–who had now been wedded (but also unhappily) for three years. "Both ladies trembled with joy and excitement as they fell into each other's arms, and were thenceforth inseparable. The man found that this friendship relation was a singular one, and hastened the departure. When the opportunity occurred, he convinced himself from the correspondence between his wife and her `friend' that their letters were exactly like those of two lovers."

It appears that the loves of such women are often very intense, and (as also in the case of male Urnings) life-long. Both classes feel themselves blessed when they love happily. Nevertheless, to many of them it is a painful fact that –in consequence of their peculiar temperament–they are, though fond of children, not in the position to found a family.

We have so far limited ourselves to some very general characteristics of the Intermediate race. It may help to clear and fix our ideas if we now describe in more detail, first, what may be called the extreme and exaggerated types of the race, and then the more normal and perfect types. By doing so we shall get a more definite and concrete view of our subject.

In the first place, then, the extreme specimens–as in most cases of extremes–are not particularly attractive, sometimes quite the reverse. In the male of this kind we have a distinctly effeminate type, sentimental, lackadaisical, mincing in gait and manners, something of a chatterbox, skilful at the needle and in woman's work, sometimes taking pleasure in dressing in woman's clothes; his figure not unfrequently betraying a tendency towards the feminine, large at the hips, supple, not muscular, the face wanting in hair, the voice inclining to be high-pitched, etc.; while his dwelling-room is orderly in the extreme, even natty, and choice of decoration and perfume. His affection, too, is often feminine in character, clinging, dependent and jealous, as of one desiring to be loved almost more than to love.

On the other hand, as the extreme type of the homogenic female, we have a rather markedly aggressive person, of strong passions, masculine manners and movements, practical in the conduct of life, sensuous rather than sentimental in love, often untidy, and outre in attire; her figure muscular, her voice rather low in pitch; her dwelling-room decorated with sporting-scenes, pistols, etc., and not without a suspicion of the fragrant weed in the atmosphere; while her love (generally to rather soft and feminine specimens of her own sex) is often a sort of furor, similar to the ordinary masculine love, and at times almost uncontrollable.

These are types which, on account of their salience, everyone will recognise more or less. Naturally, when they occur they excite a good deal of attention, and it is not an uncommon impression that most persons of the homogenic nature belong to either one or other of these classes. But in reality, of course, these extreme developments are rare, and for the most part the temperament in question is embodied in men and women of quite normal and unsensational exterior. Speaking of this subject and the connection between effeminateness and the homogenic nature in men, Dr. Moll says: "It is, however, as well to point out at the outset that effeminacy does not by any means show itself in all Urnings. Though one may find this or that indication in a great number of cases, yet it cannot be denied that a very large percentage, perhaps by far the majority of them, do not exhibit pronounced Effeminacy." And it may be supposed that we may draw the same conclusion with regard to women of this class–namely, that the majority of them do not exhibit pronounced masculine habits. In fact, while these extreme cases are of the greatest value from a scientific point of view as marking tendencies and limits of development in certain directions, it would be a serious mistake to look upon them as representative cases of the whole phases of human evolution concerned.

If now we come to what may be called the more normal type of the Uranian man, we find a man who, while possessing thoroughly masculine powers of mind and body, combines with them the tenderer and more emotional soul- nature of the woman–and sometimes to a remarkable degree. Such men, as said, are often muscular and well- built, and not distinguishable in exterior structure and the carriage of body from others of their own sex; but emotionally they are extremely complex, tender, sensitive, pitiful and loving, "full of storm and stress, of ferment and fluctuation" of the heart; the logical faculty may or may not, in their case, be well- developed, but intuition is always strong; like women they read characters at a glance, and know, without knowing how, what is passing in the minds of others; for nursing and waiting on the needs of others they have often a peculiar gift; at the bottom lies the artist- nature, with the artist's sensibility and perception. Such an one is often a dreamer, of brooding, reserved habits, often a musician, or a man of culture, courted in society, which nevertheless does not understand him– though sometimes a child of the people, without any culture, but almost always with a peculiar inborn refinement. De Joux, who speaks on the whole favourably of Uranian men and women, says of the former: "They are enthusiastic for poetry and music, are often eminently skilful in the fine arts, and are overcome with emotion and sympathy at the least sad occurrence. Their sensitiveness, their endless tenderness for children, their love of flowers, their great pity for beggars and crippled folk are truly womanly." And in another passage he indicates the artist-nature, when he says: "The nerve-system of many an Urning is the finest and the most complicated musical instrument in the service of the interior personality that can be imagined."

It would seem probable that the attachment of such an one is of a tender and profound character; indeed, it is possible that in this class of men we have the love sentiment in one of its most perfect forms–a form in which from the necessities of the situation the sensuous element, though present, is exquisitely subordinated to the spiritual. Says one writer on this subject, a Swiss, "Happy indeed is that man who has won a real Urning for his friend–he walks on roses, without ever having to fear the thorns"; and he adds, "Can there ever be a more perfect sick-nurse than an Urning?" And though these are ex parte utterances, we may believe that there is an appreciable grain of truth in them. Another writer, quoted by De Joux, speaks to somewhat the same effect, and may perhaps be received in a similar spirit. "We form," he says, "a peculiar aristocracy of modest spirits, of good and refined habit, and in many masculine circles are the representatives of the higher mental and artistic element. In us dreamers and enthusiasts lies the continual counterpoise to the sheer masculine portion of society–inclining, as it always does, to mere restless greed of gain and material sensual pleasures." That men of this kind despise women, though a not uncommon belief, is one which hardly appears to be justified. Indeed, though naturally not inclined to "fall in love" in this direction, such men are by their nature drawn rather near to women, and it would seem that they often feel a singular appreciation and understanding of the emotional needs and destinies of the other sex, leading in many cases to a genuine though what is called "Platonic" friendship. There is little doubt that they are often instinctively sought after by women, who, without suspecting the real cause, are conscious of a sympathetic chord in the homogenic which they miss in the normal man. To quote De Joux once more: "It would be a mistake to suppose that all Urnings must be woman-haters. Quite the contrary. They are not seldom the faithfulest friends, the truest allies, and most convinced defenders of women."

To come now to the more normal and perfect specimens of the homogenic woman, we find a type in which the body is thoroughly feminine and gracious, with the rondure and fulness of the female form, and the continence and aptness of its movements, but in which the inner nature is to a great extent masculine; a temperament active, brave, originative, somewhat decisive, not too emotional; fond of out-door life, of games and sports, of science, politics, or even business; good at organisation, and well-pleased with positions of responsibility, sometimes indeed making an excellent and generous leader. Such a woman, it is easily seen, from her special combination of qualities, is often fitted for remarkable work, in professional life, or as manageress of institutions, or even as ruler of a country. Her love goes out to younger and more feminine natures than her own; it is a powerful passion, almost of heroic type, and capable of inspiring to great deeds; and when held duly in leash may sometimes become an invaluable force in the teaching and training of girl-hood, or in the creation of a school of thought or action among women. Many a Santa Clara, or abbess- founder of religious houses, has probably been a woman of this type; and in all times such women–not being bound to men by the ordinary ties–have been able to work the more freely for the interests of their sex, a cause to which their own temperament impels them to devote themselves con amore.

I have now sketched–very briefly and inadequately it is true–both the extreme types and the more healthy types of the "Intermediate" man and woman: types which can be verified from history and literature, though more certainly and satisfactorily perhaps from actual life around us. And unfamiliar though the subject is, it begins to appear that it is one which modern thought and science will have to face. Of the latter and more normal types it may be said that they exist, and have always existed, in considerable abundance, and from that circumstance alone there is a strong probability that they have their place and purpose. As pointed out there is no particular indication of morbidity about them, unless the special nature of their love-sentiment be itself accounted morbid; and in the alienation of the sexes from each other, of which complaint is so often made to-day, it must be admitted that they do much to fill the gap.

102

The instinctive artistic nature of the male of this class, his sensitive spirit, his wavelike emotional temperament, combined with hardihood of intellect and body; and the frank, free nature of the female, her masculine independence and strength wedded to thoroughly feminine grace of form and manner; may be said to give them both, through their double nature, command of life in all its phases, and a certain freemasonry of the secrets of the two sexes which may well favour their function as reconcilers and interpreters. Certainly it is remarkable that some of the world's greatest leaders and artists have been dowered either wholly or in part with the Uranian temperament–as in the cases of Michel Angelo, Shakespeare, Marlowe, Alexander the Great, Julius Caesar, or, among women, Christine of Sweden, Sappho the poetess, and others.

Made in the USA
Middletown, DE
11 February 2019